THE FOOD LOVER'S GUIDE TO
PARIS

THE FOOD LOVER'S GUIDE TO
PARIS

HELEN MASSY-BERESFORD

WHITE OWL

AN IMPRINT OF PEN & SWORD BOOKS LTD.
YORKSHIRE - PHILADELPHIA

First published in Great Britain in 2019 by
PEN & SWORD WHITE OWL
An imprint of
Pen & Sword Books Ltd
Yorkshire - Philadelphia

Copyright © Helen Massy-Beresford 2019

ISBN 9781526733696

Printed and bound by Replika Press Pvt. Ltd.
Design: Paul Wilkinson.

Pen & Sword Books Limited incorporates the imprints
of Atlas, Archaeology, Aviation, Discovery, Family
History, Fiction, History, Maritime, Military, Military
Classics, Politics, Select, Transport, True Crime, Air
World, Frontline Publishing, Leo Cooper, Remember
When, Seaforth Publishing, The Praetorian Press,
Wharncliffe Local History, Wharncliffe Transport,
Wharncliffe True Crime and White Owl.

For a complete list of Pen & Sword titles please contact
PEN & SWORD BOOKS LIMITED
47 Church Street, Barnsley, South Yorkshire, S70 2AS,
United Kingdom
E-mail: enquiries@pen-and-sword.co.uk
Website: www.pen-and-sword.co.uk

Or
PEN AND SWORD BOOKS
1950 Lawrence Rd, Havertown, PA 19083, USA
E-mail: Uspen-and-sword@casematepublishers.com
Website: www.penandswordbooks.com

CONTENTS

1

INTRODUCTION

PARIS HAS BEEN considered the gastronomic capital of the world since the dawn of the modern era, when the forerunners of today's tourists began travelling for pleasure and reporting back on the quirks and highlights of their destinations.

Parisian cuisine had been evolving for hundreds of years before then, taking on board influences from as far back as Ancient Rome and incorporating them into its own culinary tradition. It was only in the late nineteenth century however, when the first of the city's famous brasseries opened their doors, that classics of French cuisine such as a simple steak-frites served with a glass of red, an elaborate array of mussels, whelks, prawns and oysters served on a platter piled high with ice, a perfectly caramelised tarte tatin – began to be so closely associated with the Parisian dining experience.

Fast forward just over a hundred years though, and Paris's top ranking in the culinary world has been threatened for a variety of reasons; health-conscious diners favouring the fresher, lighter flavours of olive-oil dominated Italian cuisine over the perception of traditional French dishes being full of cream and butter; culinary revolutions in other European cities, such as London and Copenhagen, drawing gourmet travellers away to new restaurant experiences and complacency among the city's restaurateurs. Confident of a constant stream of hungry travellers passing through their doors (Paris is the world's most visited tourist destination) standards slipped, with some restaurants abandoning the fresh ingredients for which French food is famous, in favour of bought-in frozen versions of popular dishes.

When France pushed for the inclusion of French cuisine, or more specifically a traditional French multi-course gastronomic meal, with all its attendant ceremony and ritual, on UNESCO's Intangible Cultural Heritage list in 2010 it was seen by many as a doomed attempt to promote a stuffy, over-formal cuisine that, although world-renowned, was not adapting to a changing world.

Perhaps it was a wake-up call. In the last couple of decades, Paris has been undergoing its own culinary revolution. For a city whose

origins date back over two millennia, assimilating outside influences is to be expected, but in keeping with an increasingly globalised and interconnected world, Paris has been embracing far-flung food influences with much greater enthusiasm than in the past. Many of the top chefs making their mark in Paris today combine French cuisine with another country's culinary tradition.

Vegetarians and vegans who, even a decade ago, were greeted with

barely disguised horror or outright disbelief in many a Parisian bistrot, are now well catered for. Small plates and tapas-style eating are all the rage and seen as an acceptable alternative to a formal three-course affair.

The quintessentially Parisian cafés are still going strong but a new wave of young entrepreneurs has brought a variety and quality of coffee to the city that was previously lacking and is serving it in more relaxed surroundings. As in other major cities around the world, Parisians have embraced the local food movement – from beer brewed in Paris to the city's first cheese producer and rooftop beehives and vegetable gardens.

This renewed interest highlights some of the principles that have ensured that French and Parisian cuisine are still world-renowned; when it comes to the food itself, it's all about choosing high-quality ingredients, knowing where they come from and enjoying them in season. The rituals surrounding eating are vitally important too – while Paris is now undoubtedly embracing the takeaway culture and a more casual street-food style, it has taken much longer than in some of its neighbouring countries.

For the French, sitting down and really enjoying what you're eating is vital. Being 'gourmand' – liking your food – is seen as a good thing in France – sitting down to a four-(or more) course meal including cheese and dessert for a special occasion, but equally making sure you sit and enjoy your sandwich and soup during your office lunch break, is all part of a balanced approach to eating that for now at least is still the basis of French food culture.

Many of the millions of tourists who visit Paris every year will have high on their holiday wish list experiences such as tasting the perfect snails in garlic butter, struggling to choose between the intricate cakes laid out in the window of a pâtisserie or simply sipping strong black coffee at a pavement café. This book aims to guide you through those unmissable Parisian gourmet moments as well as showing you how much more the city's food scene has to offer.

Brasserie Francœur.
Helen Massy-Beresford

lafourchette.com
129 Rue Caulaincourt
75018

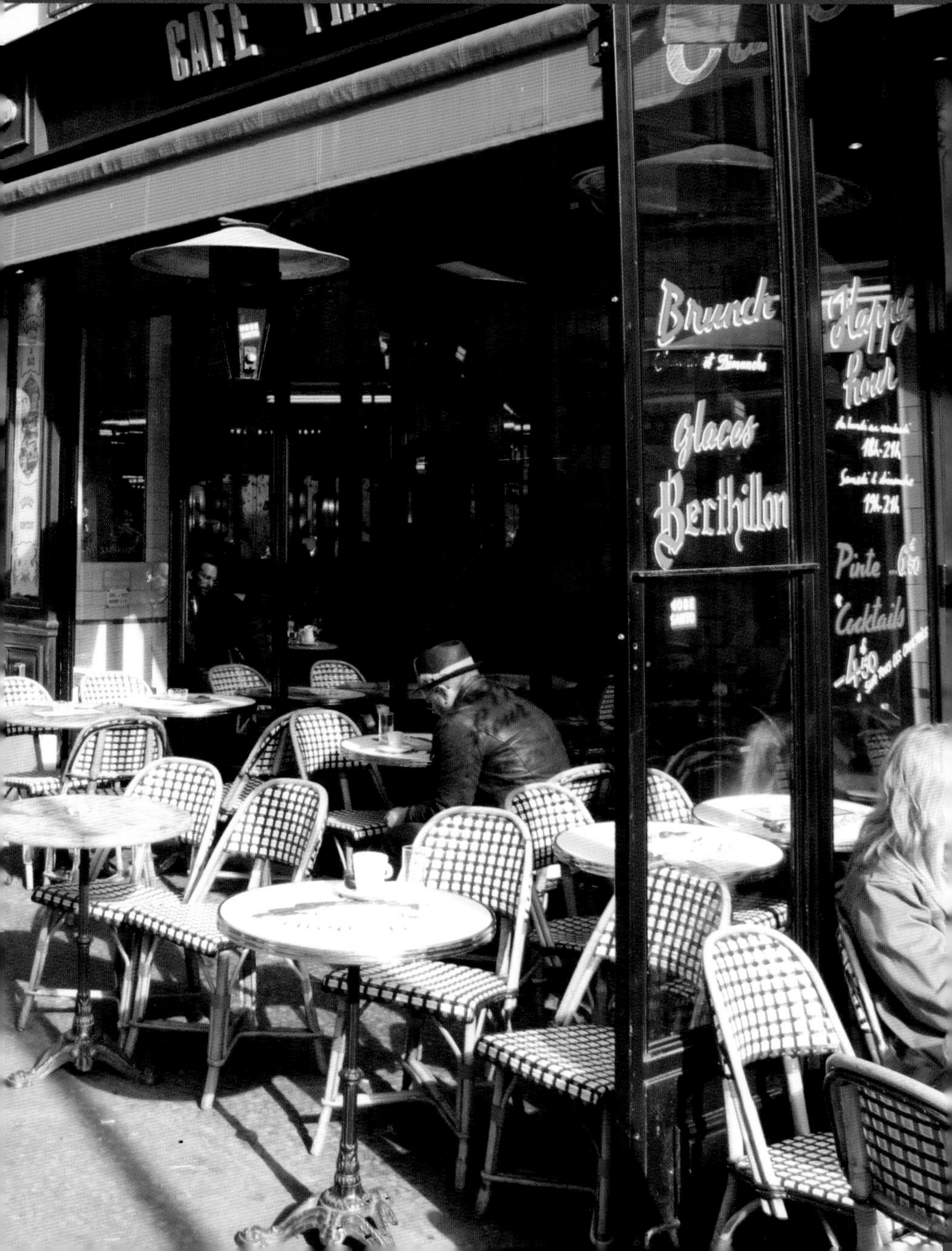
CAFE
Brunch
Glaces
Berthillon
Happy hour
Pinte
Cocktails

Establishments in the Paris arrondissements

1ST ARRONDISSEMENT
- La Dame de Pic
- Le Zimmer
- Hôtel Costes
- Pirouette
- Le Meurice
- Au Pied de Cochon
- L'Escargot Montorgueil
- Macéo
- Bar Hemingway
- La Régalade
- Juveniles
- Café Blanc
- Willi's Wine Bar
- L'Absinthe
- Restaurant du Palais Royal
- Café Kitsuné
- Café Marly
- Veget'Halles
- Lemoni Café
- Foucade
- Cantine California
- Le Fumoir
- Le Nemours
- Café Verlet
- Baguett's Café
- Le Café des Initiés
- Comptoir des Abbayes
- Le Marché Saint-Honoré
- La Cave des Tuileries
- Le Marché Saint-Eustache – Les Halles
- Senoble
- Pierre Marcolini
- Sébastien Gaudard
- Angelina
- Olio Pane Vino
- yam'Tcha
- Yasube
- JanTchi
- Djakarta Bali
- Nodaiwa

2ND ARRONDISSEMENT
- Le Mesturet
- Aux Lyonnais
- Le Grand Colbert
- Le Moderne
- Frenchie
- Habemus
- Un Jour à Peyrassol
- Dépôt Légal
- Le Pas Sage
- La Grille Montorgueil
- Drouant
- Noglu
- JANINE loves SUNDAY
- Sur un Arbre Perché
- La Pascade
- Cojean
- Matamata Coffee
- Le Vaudeville
- Ma Cave Fleury
- La Fermette
- Kodama
- Maison Stohrer
- Fou de Pâtisserie
- 37m2
- Entre 2 Rives
- Daroco
- Hang-A-Ri

3RD ARRONDISSEMENT
- Chez Jenny
- L'Estaminet
- L'Ambassade d'Auvergne
- Breizh Café
- Café Crème
- Café de la Poste
- Café Suedois
- Hank Pizza
- Hank Burger
- Le Potager du Marais
- Saucette
- Pontochoux Paris
- Neighbours

- Loustic
- Boot Café
- 7 au Marais
- La Maison Plisson
- Breizh Café Épicerie
- Le Barav
- Le Marché des Enfants Rouges
- Pain de Sucre
- Popelini
- Jacques Genin
- Okomusu
- Grazie

4TH ARRONDISSEMENT
- Bofinger
- Chez Julien
- La Brasserie du Pied de Fouet
- Le Café Français
- Le Trumilou
- Gaspard de la Nuit
- Le Café Livres
- Au Petit Fer à Cheval
- Les Fous de l'Île
- Bistrot de l'Oulette
- Berthillon
- Le Grand Cœur
- Café Ginger
- Le Grand Appetit
- EAT Gluten Free
- Artefact
- Dans Le Noir
- The Grilled Cheese Factory
- Le Peloton
- La Caféothèque
- Mamy Thérèse
- Terres de Café
- À la Ville de Rodez
- Comme à Lisbonne
- La Cuisine Paris
- L'Éclair de Génie

- Pâtisserie Michalak
- Yann Couvreur
- La Boutique Jaune – Sacha Finkelsztajn
- Miznon
- Chez Marianne
- L'As du Fallafel

5TH ARRONDISSEMENT
- La Tour d'Argent
- Brasserie Balzar
- Le Pré Verre
- Café de la Nouvelle Mairie
- Verse Toujours
- Cave La Bourgogne
- Le Restaurant de la Grande Mosquée de Paris
- Le Salon du Panthéon
- Vegan Folie's
- Le Grenier de Nôtre Dame
- Coco de Mer
- Le Bonbon au Palais
- Au Thé Gourmand
- Strada
- Café Shakespeare & Company
- Café Léa
- Brewberry
- Androuet
- Golosino
- Les Belles Envies
- Carl Marletti
- La Maison des Tartes
- Eric Kayser
- Godjo
- Le Lhassa

6TH ARRONDISSEMENT
- Restaurant Guy Savoy
- Le Procope
- Brasserie Lipp
- Bouillon Racine

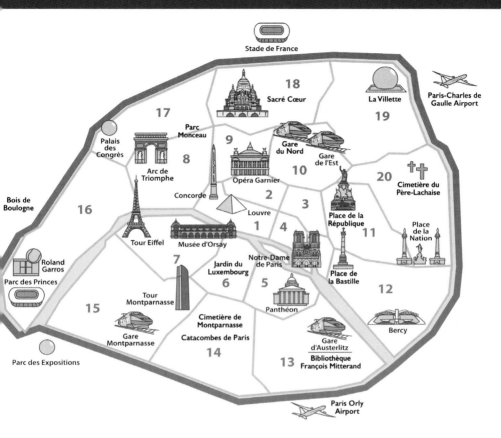

- L'Avant Comptoir du Marché
- La Lozère
- Crêperie du Vieux Journal
- La Charette Créole
- Le Comptoir du Relais
- La Table du Luxembourg
- La Closerie des Lilas
- Huguette Bistro de la Mer
- Hot Vog
- Sense Eat
- Paradis Marguerite
- Frappé by Bloom

- Coffee Club
- Le Rostand
- Café de Flore
- Les Deux Magots
- Le Select
- Treize Bakery Paris
- Marché Saint-Germain
- Da Rosa
- La Crèmerie
- Maison Bremond
- Pierre Hermé
- Arnaud Larher
- Chez Bebert
- Happy Days Diner

7TH ARRONDISSEMENT
- Le Jules Verne/Le 58 Tour Eiffel
- Le Grand Bistro de Breteuil
- Les Fables de la Fontaine
- Le Pertinence
- Café Constant
- L'Ami Jean
- Café du Marché
- Clover
- Divellec
- Le Basilic
- Cuillier

- Coutume
- La Grande Épicerie de Paris
- Mariage Frères
- Truffes Folie
- Henri Le Roux
- Debauve & Gallais
- Marlon
- Nagi

8TH ARRONDISSEMENT
- Le Grand Restaurant
- Le Taillevent
- Les 110 de Taillevent
- Apicius

- Le Cinq
- Brasserie Mollard
- MINIPALAIS
- Les Koupoles
- À l'Affiche
- Le Colibri
- Flora Danica
- L'Orangerie
- Bloom Penthièvre
- Les Bols de Jean
- Le Camion Qui Fume
- Honor
- Bread & Roses
- Maille
- La New Cave
- Fauchon
- Les Caves Augé
- Ladurée
- Taisho Ken
- Thu Thu 8e
- L'Étoile Marocaine

9TH ARRONDISSEMENT
- Café de la Paix
- Le Bouillon Chartier
- Orties
- Le Pantruche
- La Petite Bretonne
- L'Élan 9
- J'Go
- Musée de la Vie Romantique
- Bül – Bar à Cannes
- Helmut Newcake
- Laélo
- Popotes Cantine Respectueuse
- 42 Degrés
- Privé de Dessert
- Picto
- Soucoupe
- KB CaféShop
- Rose Bakery
- Le Printemps du Goût
- La Parisienne
- Lafayette Gourmet
- RAP Épicerie
- Beillevaire
- La Maison du Miel
- Marché Anvers
- Aurore Capucine

- A La Mère de Famille
- Mesdemoiselles Madeleines
- Gallika
- Peco Peco
- Pink Mamma
- Holy Bol

10TH ARRONDISSEMENT
- Le Galopin
- Bouillon Julien
- La Strasbourgeoise
- Hôtel du Nord
- Terminus
- Bistro Basque
- Chez Michel
- Chez Casimir
- Chez Prune
- L'Atmosphère
- Café A
- Pink Flamingo
- Point Ephemère – Le Top
- Jules et Shim
- Café Pinson
- Bob's Juice Bar
- Apéro Saint-Martin
- Pancake Sisters
- BOL
- La Pointe du Grouin
- Holybelly
- Chez Jeannette
- La Sardine
- Marché Saint-Quentin
- Le Verre Volé
- Du Pain et des Idées
- Mamagoto
- Ravioli Chinois Nord-Est
- Krishna Bhavan
- Le Petit Cambodge
- La Madonnina
- The Sunken Chip
- Le Bistrot Mme Shawn

11TH ARRONDISSEMENT
- Le Chateaubriand
- Septime
- Le Beau Marché
- Monsieur Edgar
- Le Bistrot du Peintre
- Clamato
- Le Pure Café

- Le Perchoir
- Al Taglio
- GreenHouse
- Bears and Raccoons
- Chambelland
- SOYA
- ChezAline
- Jones
- Le Food Market
- Fulgurances
- Ten Belles Bread
- Café Charbon
- Marché Père Lachaise
- Épicerie Et Associés
- Le Vin Qui Parle
- Blue Elephant
- La Bague de Kenza
- L'Équateur
- Acqua e Farina
- Café Titon

12TH ARRONDISSEMENT
- Le Train Bleu
- Le Square Trousseau
- Table
- Amarante
- Le Chalet des Îles Daumesnil
- Scotta
- Gentle Gourmet
- Comptoir Veggie
- Marché Beauvau (marché d'Aligre)
- Curry Street
- Gourmet Gourmand
- Aux Merveilleux de Fred
- Bar à Momos
- Le Touareg

13TH ARRONDISSEMENT
- Au Petit Marguéry Rive Gauche
- Chez Gladines
- Des Crêpes et des Cailles
- Simone
- Les Temps des Cerises
- L'Incubateur de Fraîcheur
- Season Square
- Tooq Tooq
- New Soul Food
- La Brigade
- La Felicità

- L'Arobase Café
- Le Merle Moqueur
- Tang Frères
- Les Abeilles
- Gérard Mulot
- Laurent Duchêne
- Pho Banh Cuon 14
- Délices de Shandong
- Xinh Xinh
- Tricotin

14TH ARRONDISSEMENT
- La Coupole
- Le Zeyer
- Les Fauves
- Origins 14
- La Crêperie de Josselin
- Le Pavillon Montsouris
- Raw Cakes
- Auto Passion Café
- Café Daguerre
- Hexagone Café
- Accordéon Paris Gourmands
- O Sole Mio
- Fromagerie Vacroux
- Dominique Saibron
- Chez Bogato
- Ayako-Teppanyaki
- Un Jour à Hà Nôi

15TH ARRONDISSEMENT
- Le Café du Commerce
- Ciel de Paris
- Brasserie Lola
- La Villa Corse
- Le Troquet
- L'Os à Moelle
- L'Accolade
- Chat Mallows Café
- O Coffeeshop
- Café Beaugrenelle
- Marché Grenelle
- Fromagerie Laurent Dubois
- Oliviers & Co
- Sadaharu Aoki
- Des Gâteaux et du Pain – Claire Damon
- Poîlane
- Le Concert de Cuisine

- Cô Tu'
- Les Délices du Maroc

16TH ARRONDISSEMENT
- Masha
- Comice
- Le Petit Pergolèse
- Le Brandevin
- La Causerie
- Le Chalet des Îles
- La Grande Cascade
- L'Oiseau Blanc
- Le Pré Catelan
- Bustronome
- Le Coffee Parisien
- La Rotonde de la Muette
- Delizius
- La Grande Épicerie
- Faye Paris
- La Pâtisserie Cyril Lignac
- Shang Palace
- Fuxia
- LiLi

17TH ARRONDISSEMENT
- Chez Georges
- Le Refuge des Moines
- Le Bouchon et l'Assiette
- Crêpe Cœur
- Le P'tit Musset
- L'Envie du Jour
- Le Bistrot des Dames
- Terrasse 17
- Little Nonna
- Maca'rong
- Super Vegan
- MyLO Concept Store
- Le Costaud des Batignolles
- Dose
- Le Monceau
- Maison Castro
- Au Bout Du Champ
- L'AtrYum des Saveurs
- Marché couvert Batignolles
- Acide Macaron
- La Romainville
- Harpers
- Liberic
- Mamma Roma

- Maison Aname
- Ménélik

18TH ARRONDISSEMENT
- Café Francœur
- Brasserie Barbès
- Chez Foucher Mère et Fille
- Patakrep
- Les Routiers
- Polissons
- Les Trois Frères
- Bouillon Pigalle
- Café Miroir
- Fichon
- Chez Francis La Butte
- Le Lamarck
- La Vieille Pie
- La REcyclerie
- Kiez Biergarten
- Musée de Montmartre – Jardins Renoir
- L'Abattoir Végétal
- Le Très Particulier
- Lord Of Barbès Gin
- Le Bal Café Otto
- Café Pimpin
- Café Lomi
- The Hardware Société
- Soul Kitchen
- La Laiterie de Paris
- Marché couvert de la Chapelle (marché de l'Olive)
- En Vrac
- Brasserie de la Goutte d'Or
- Fromagerie Lepic
- Pain Pain
- La Rose de Tunis
- Le Dibi
- Tim La Princesse
- New Thai San
- Thu Thu
- Café Léon

19TH ARRONDISSEMENT
- Au Boeuf Couronné
- Le Laumière
- Café Bolivar
- Quedubon
- Le Bastringue

- Rosa Bonheur
- Le Pavillon Puebla
- Kiez Kanal
- Paname Brewing Company
- Bar Ourcq
- La Petite Halle
- Le CENTQUATRE-PARIS
- Biiim
- Le Pavillon des Canaux
- Le Bellerive
- Halle Sécretan
- La Cave de Belleville
- La Vieille France
- Poîlane
- Guo Xin
- Le Pacifique
- Itegue Taitu
- Mian Guan
- Bombay Curry

20TH ARRONDISSEMENT
- Les Canailles Ménilmontant
- Le Bistro du Parisien
- Les Allobroges
- Café Le Papillon
- Le Grand Bain
- Le Petit 20e
- Dilia
- Le Comptoir
- Le Jourdain
- Les Triplettes
- Aux Petits Oignons
- Moncœur Belleville
- Mama Shelter
- Love me cru
- Primeur
- Le Mezze du Chef
- Chez Elle
- La Halle Aux Oliviers – La Bellevilloise
- La Mère Lachaise
- Aux Folies Belleville
- La Laverie
- Maison Landemaine
- L'Épicerie Ô Divin
- Demoncy-Vergne
- Le 140
- Wen Zhou
- Chez Younice

2

BON APPETIT, A HOW-TO GUIDE

PARIS WAITERS HAVE a largely undeserved reputation for being unfriendly, snooty and even downright rude. Although I have had the odd bad experience, when people complain about Parisian waiting staff I always think of the waiter in a nondescript café near the Gare du Nord, who offered to either cut up my croque monsieur for me or hold my baby while I did it (I managed on my own but very much appreciated the offer). It is fair to say that they can be brusque, often because they're busy, but some basic tips can smooth the interaction.

Say 'bonjour'. Or 'bonsoir': this is vitally important and not just in restaurants. Wherever you go in Paris, into a shop, gallery, restaurant, café or any other place where you cross paths with a member of staff, say 'bonjour' – omitting to do it is rude and will get you off on the wrong foot. Ninety percent of the bad feeling that can arise between Parisian waiting staff and their non-Francophone customers can be traced back to this initial misunderstanding. But don't be offended if your waiter replies in English. Some 35 million tourists pass through Paris and the Île de France region every year – nearly all waiters will speak at least the basics needed to communicate with their customers and many much more. Menus are very often available in English. To get a waiter's attention in a busy restaurant, under no circumstances should you shout 'garçon' – this is very old-fashioned and quite rude. A simple 's'il vous plaît' should do the trick.

Leave a small tip. A sizeable tip is not necessary as service is included in your bill. However, leaving the small change if you've paid in cash, or an extra euro, two or three depending on the size of your bill is always welcome.

Know where you're going... A brasserie is usually open all hours, serving the French classics – a variety of steaks, choucroute, seafood platters, confit duck as well as salads and a selection of daily specials. In the more traditional, well-known brasseries, the décor is often

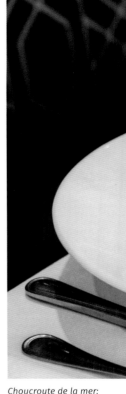

Choucroute de la mer: a La Coupole classic.
Yann Deret

grand, with an art nouveau feel, but while these are not the most expensive places to eat out in Paris, with main courses often around the €20 mark, once you add in wine, coffees and side dishes, it can soon add up.

Many of the more run-of-the-mill street corner cafés also style themselves brasseries too – they may have pavement tables, drinks and a more limited menu of snack-type food or plats du jour.

Bistrots, with an ever-changing menu depending on the ingredients to hand, are often much cheaper, especially if you choose the set menu of two or three courses, sometimes including a glass of wine and/or coffee too for a fixed price, which are often available only at lunchtime or on weekdays. The spaces are often smaller, with tables tightly crammed in and spilling out onto the pavement in the summer months.

Lili

J-F Mallet

Fine dining at LiLi (top left) and La Dame de Pic (above).

At the other end of the scale, fine-dining and especially Michelin-starred restaurants are often the most formal of all, although without the grandiose décor that signifies a brasserie. Prices, while varying widely depending on quality and location, are generally higher than either bistrot or brasserie.

...And when. While legendary long French lunches with three courses and wine may now be rare on weekdays at least, Parisians still like to take their time over their midday break. Cafés and restaurants often offer a good value 'formule' or set menu deal at lunchtime, two or three courses with coffee and/or a glass of wine that will arrive quickly to accommodate workers on their lunch break. In the evening, Parisians tend to eat late, with dinner rarely before 8 p.m. and often more like 9 p.m. Most restaurants open at 7 p.m. but you're likely to be the only diners at that time. While most restaurants and bistrots will stop serving around 10.30 p.m. and have a clearly defined lunch service (often between 12.00 noon and 2.30 p.m.) brasseries and cafés have much more flexible hours, with some even open round the clock.

Although France is gradually embracing the concept of snacking (the French word is 'grignoter'), eating three meals a day (four for children) and nothing in between is still seen as the norm – and the best way to eat.

Have brunch. Paris has been enthusiastically embracing the concept of brunch for a few years now. Many of the rising number of cafés and restaurants serving weekend brunch propose a 'formule' or brunch deal: prices can be anything from about €15 to upwards of €30 and the selection will usually include a hot drink, a fresh juice and a pastry. That can then be supplemented with almost anything – a main dish from the menu or a more obviously brunch-style dish such as

Brunch at Pancake Sisters.
Pancake Sisters

eggs, avocado on toast or a bagel, a salad, some homemade biscuits or cake, a fruit salad, granola with yoghurt ... there are no rules. For brunchers used to a more limited selection of bacon, eggs, pancakes and the like, the combination of roast chicken, coffee and a pain au chocolat can be slightly odd.

Book ahead. In all but the most casual cafés a quick phone call will usually secure your table and avoid disappointment or a lengthy queue.

Tchin-tchin (cheers!) An apéritif or apéro is traditionally a pre-dinner (or lunch) drink said to stimulate the appetite, often served with a small dish of olives, peanuts or similar.

The Parisian way to drink beer is by the 'demi' – literally a 'half', but in fact a 250ml measure. If you don't mind what beer you're getting (in a standard bar or café this will usually be Kronenbourg or its slightly more upmarket sister 1664) you can just order a 'demi'. Confusingly, to order a half-litre, ask for 'une pinte' (a pint).

Pack a picnic. If weather permits, gathering the ingredients for a Parisian picnic is one of the city's great food experiences: the perfect crunchy baguette, ripe Camembert, garlicky sausage, and depending on the season, flavourful tomatoes, gariguette strawberries or white peaches. Be sure to check your chosen park allows visitors to access the grass – many don't; but the Parc des Buttes-Chaumont, the Parc Monceau and slightly further out the Bois de Vincennes and the Bois de Boulogne are good picnic spots.

Yann Deret

'Fait maison'. As a response to a perceived decline in quality in Paris restaurant food, and to fight back against the rise of pre-prepared industrial food being served up to diners, French authorities launched a campaign to highlight homemade food. Restaurants that make their food from fresh ingredients on site can signal this by displaying a logo – a saucepan with the roof of a house for a lid – or the words 'fait maison'.

(No) smoking. An unhappy side effect of the ban on smoking indoors is that terraces – often covered and heated in winter – have become default smoking areas.

No room for pudding? A café or thé gourmand is the particularly civilised concept of having a coffee or tea served with two or three small sweet morsels such as a mini-macaron, tiny crème brûlée and bite-sized chocolate cake.

Monday blues. A lot of shops, cafés, bars and restaurants have a weekly rest-day on Mondays, while some take Tuesdays or Wednesdays and many shops close on Sundays, so if you've set your heart on somewhere particular check the opening hours in advance.

3

WHERE, WHEN AND HOW – A GUIDE TO DIFFERENT VENUES

Pure Paris

With their gilt-and-mirrors Art Nouveau décor, bow-tied waiters wielding enormous trays, and crisp white tablecloths, Paris's famous brasseries are as much a part of the city's aesthetic as the regimented boulevards with their wrought iron balustrades, the little cobbled alleyways and the broad sweeps of the Seine. They're also a little piece of living history with menus full of Frencher-than-French classics and often beer on tap, reflecting their origins – the word 'brasserie' means brewery and many were founded in the late nineteenth century by refugees from Alsace which had been annexed by Germany.

Grandiose surroundings at Le Grand Colbert.

   The best ones conjure up a Paris of days gone by in all their Belle Époque glory and have provided a backdrop to Paris's cultural and political life ever since. Coco Chanel and Jean Cocteau were among the regulars at Le Train Bleu, while everyone from Josephine Baker with her pet cheetah to Simone de Beauvoir and Jean-Paul Sartre visited La Coupole, another Paris institution. More recently, Emmanuel Macron was criticised for celebrating his first round victory in the 2017 presidential election by treating his staff to dinner at

Yann Deret

La Rotonde – the move was seen as premature and flashy and reminiscent of Nicolas Sarkozy who celebrated his own presidential win years earlier in the upmarket Fouquet's.

Relax in the cosy atmosphere of leather banquettes and dark wood panels in Bofinger, the city's oldest brasserie, or enjoy the dissonance of stepping from the crowded concourse of the Gare de Lyon station into a majestic space of over-the-top chandeliers, gilt and frescos: Le Train Bleu.

No one visits a brasserie to be surprised by the originality of the menu, but whether it's buttery, garlicky snails, a simple entrecôte, the classic brasserie choice of a seafood platter,

Au Pied de Cochon.

a choucroute garnie or a rum baba, the quality is generally good, and the outlandish décor and the theatre of the black-and-white attired waiters are as much a part of the brasserie experience as the classics à la carte.

Beyond the brasseries, for a formal dining experience with originality and modernity to boot, you've come to the right city. Even if chefs and restaurants in other major cities across the globe now challenge France's dominance, the City of Light is still the spiritual home of fine dining.

The famous wine cellar at La Tour d'Argent.
Thomas Renaut

Pirouette. Pirouette Aimery Chemin

Le Pré Catelan. Richard Haughton

Bistrot classics.

Le Bistro du Parisien.
Le Bistro du Parisien

Best Bistrots

At the other end of the scale from the Michelin stars and candelabra-ed brasseries, with chalkboards of daily specials, crammed-in tables and carafes of wine – even if the traditional red check tablecloth is pretty rare these days – the bistrot is generally a much more casual affair, though just as Parisian an experience. If you go for a weekday lunch deal a bistrot can be a great way to sample traditional French fare for a moderate price.

Beginning in the 1990s, the 'bistronomy' movement – gastronomic food without the formality – has seen energetic young chefs bring together the charm and casual atmosphere of the traditional bistrot with a focus on high-quality seasonal and often local ingredients and skilled cooking at moderate prices with a decent wine list – all with a dash of originality thrown in. Simple and sometimes long-forgotten ingredients are given their chance to shine, with innovative twists on old-fashioned dishes or techniques, or flavours borrowed from foreign cuisines brought to bear on French classics. In a mark of how seriously the city takes the blend of traditional and modern, casual and high-skilled that is bistronomy, the Paris mayor's office publishes a list of its top 100 bistrots.

La Causerie. La Causerie

Orties. Nicolas Maday

Dining in Paris is a great way to explore some of the distinct identities of the French regions: Espelette-pepper-spiked sausages from the Basque Country or nutty buckwheat galettes from Brittany, creamy flammeküche from Alsace or olivey sun-soaked pissaladière from Nice would seem to have originated in different worlds, not different corners of the same country.

Many of these diverse influences are apparent in Paris's restaurant scene, either as regional establishments or having found their way on to the chalkboard of 'Parisian' classics in their own right.

The Auvergne area of central France, with its volcanic landscapes and lush pastures, has had a particularly strong influence on Parisian food over the decades thanks to the influx of large numbers of people from this and the surrounding Lozère and Aveyron areas unable to survive in rural France. Looking for work in the city during the nineteenth and twentieth centuries, many of them ended up running bistrots. Their presence can still be felt in popular dishes like Salers beef or sausage with aligot, a rich concoction of mashed potato blended with garlic, cream and tomme fraîche cheese.

If you're keen to discover the cuisine from a particular region of Paris, one way to find plenty of choice is to head to the railway station that serves that part of the country, as traditionally the migrants from those areas set up around their 'home' station. For crêpes and galettes from Brittany try the area around the Gare du Montparnasse, while for Alsatian and eastern French specialities try the streets around the Gare de l'Est.

Al Fresco Paris

Paris may be famous for the pavement cafés you'll find on every corner, but some of the best fresco locations are to be found away from the traffic-clogged streets – if you know where to look. In Europe's most densely-populated city, the parks provide a much-needed breath of air, as well as an array of food choices.

The Parc des Buttes-Chaumont, with its Italianate temple

Moncœur Belleville. Moncoeur Belleville

Café tables on the rue Mouffetard. Helen Massy-Beresford

perched on a craggy outcrop, would be at home in a fairy tale.
A former quarry landscaped into a hilly park in the nineteenth
century, it's popular with joggers and picnickers alike as one
of the few Paris parks in which the grass is not out of bounds
and is also home to some of the city's loveliest al fresco
eating and drinking spots.

The canals and reservoir in north eastern Paris, including
the Bassin de la Villette and the Canal Saint-Martin – whose
green metal bridges are famous for featuring in the film
Amélie – were once busy commercial waterways but now offer
a welcome sense of space in a densely built up corner of the
city, with shady plane trees, no shortage of café terraces and
many takeaway options to be enjoyed along the banks of the
canal.

In tourist-thronged Montmartre you can escape the crowds
and even get a breath of fresh air in hidden gardens, while
on the banks of the Seine the Esplanade des Invalides is a
huge expanse of grass you are actually allowed to walk and

*Shopping for fresh
seafood.*

even picnic on, with the spectacular backdrop of the Invalides military monument and museum and the ostentatious gilded Pont Alexandre III in front. On the Île Saint-Louis, Parisians pick up an ice cream from the legendary Berthillon and sit by the banks of the Seine.

On the left bank (south of the Seine river) the shady courtyard of the Grande Mosquée (Paris's main mosque) is the perfect rest stop after a morning stalking the galleries of the nearby Muséum national d'Histoire Naturelle (natural history museum) and exploring the Jardin des Plantes (botanical gardens).

Market streets like the rue Mouffetard, the rue Daguerre and the rue des Martyrs are picnickers' paradises lined with top cheesemongers, wine merchants, fruit and veg stalls and delicatessens.

Parks like the parc Monceau in the 8th and the Jardin du Luxembourg in the sixth are perfect picnic spots – though be warned, you won't always be able to spread your picnic rug out on the grass: the 'pelouse interdite' (keep off the grass) signs are strictly policed.

Going Green

'Lunch kills one half of Paris, dinner the other,' wrote the eighteenth-century writer and philosopher Charles de Montesquieu. Up until recently, he had a point. Heavy sauces, huge hunks of meat and vegetables either notable by their absence or cooked beyond recognition, were the norm in many of the more old-fashioned Parisian eateries.

Announcing that you were vegetarian in the Paris of the 1980s or 1990s might be met with a shrug or a look of incomprehension from your waiter, or worse – the insistence that a dish was vegetarian – 'just a few lardons'... At best there would be the offer of a plate of chips.

All that has changed, with Paris embracing all manner of healthy-eating trends. What started out as a niche movement has amplified rapidly, and the city, especially in its younger and more bohemian corners, is dotted with gluten-free

Hank

Big Man

bakeries, juice bars, organic shops and vegetarian and even vegan restaurants. Call it 'hipsterisation' or globalisation – many of the veggie and vegan, green and healthy highlights either borrow from other cuisines or are run by non-French chefs – but cafés and restaurants serving up fresh, healthy food, always with a Parisian twist, are a welcome addition to the City of Light's formerly rather heavy food scene.

In the land of the croissant and the baguette, gluten-free eating is a challenge, but cafés and restaurants are increasingly wising up to the demand for alternatives.

One very French and very traditional option for gluten-free diners is a galette or savoury pancake, because if made from the traditional buckwheat flour used in Brittany these are naturally gluten-free, depending on the fillings of course. It's worth checking to make sure that your choice really is 'sans gluten', but crêperies are a surprisingly good bet for those avoiding gluten. The sweet dessert crêpes do contain standard wheat flour, however.

Fresh, healthy and free-from options are increasingly popular in Paris.

La REcyclerie

SOYA

Pop-Up Paris

Eating out in Paris is not just about bow-tied waiters or red-and-white-checked tablecloths. Although Paris clings more rigidly to some dining traditions than other cities, in recent years there has been a shake-up of the food and drink scene.

Parisians have embraced some of the food trends that have swept through other cities in recent years – food trucks have become popular and the gourmet burger is as ubiquitous on Parisian menus as it is in New York or London.

But pop-ups, by definition, are ephemeral, so the Pop-Up category in this book will explore both these constantly changing dining experiences as well as the more inventive and unusual end of the city's vast selection of permanent restaurants, bistrots and bars. These are the dining

Parisisan pizza: the pizza van at CENTQUATRE-PARIS and La Felicità (right). Martin Argyroglo

Jérôme Galland

experiences that have the power to make you laugh, or question what you thought you knew about eating out in Paris, the best areas of the city to head to for a laid-back vibe as well as the food trucks and casual hang-outs that have shown their staying power despite their pop-up origins.

Café Culture

Think of a Parisian café and you probably conjure up something very like the Café de Flore, on the boulevard de Saint-Germain in the 6th arrondissement, one of the city's oldest coffeehouses (dating back to 1887) and a true Parisian institution. From the black-and-white clad harried waiters to its associations with world-famous French writers, artists and intellectuals of the twentieth century (Albert Camus, Simone de Beauvoir, Jean-Paul Sartre and Brigitte Bardot have all been among its regulars at one time or another), the terrace tables perfect for people-watching, and the red geraniums lining the awning, it's got it all. The coffee itself is by no means the star attraction. In fact, surprisingly often in this food- and ingredient-obsessed city, the standard of coffee can be disappointing, with bitter robusta blends from one of a handful of big suppliers the usual fare in many cafés.

Luckily for Parisians, their Antipodean friends have come to the rescue, with a wave of Australian-influenced (and often run) cafés spearheading a caffeine revolution in recent years that has broadened out into a trend for casual all-day eateries with simple but good quality menus and crucially, top quality coffee. Single estate blends served on rough wooden tables alongside granola or avocado toast may be in some ways a depressing symbol of globalisation, but when it comes to improving the quality of their morning brew, Parisians have much to thank hipsters for.

Outside the bobo enclaves, Parisians' coffee of choice is usually an espresso or an an espresso with a dash of milk – a 'noisette'. Café allongé is an espresso diluted with hot water. Café crème or café au lait is considered a breakfast drink only. A request for one after a meal will be met, but may be delivered with a sigh. A déca is a decaffeinated coffee – if you simply order a déca it will be a decaffeinated espresso.

In a traditional French café you'll have the choice between taking your coffee on the terrace, at a table or at the bar, where it will usually cost less. More recent arrivals on the Parisian café scene won't necessarily make this distinction and are more likely to offer takeaway options, a request still often met with pure incomprehension in the more traditional cafés.

Do It Yourself

You can find small shops selling good quality ingredients in every corner of the city – bakeries drawing you in with the smell of fresh-baked sourdough; the cool mustiness of speciality fromagers (cheesemongers) where you'll be encouraged to try before you buy and guided through the subtleties affecting the taste of each huge block of comté or

Paris is a cheese lover's paradise.

tomme or wine merchants who'll want to know what you're eating before they suggest an accompaniment. But some areas of the city lend themselves in particular to a leisurely morning of picnic shopping – a handful or ripe tomatoes here, a little pot of aromatic olives there, a generous wedge of brie there. Whatever you're shopping for, take your time and chat to the stallholder or shop assistant.

If you're buying a bottle of wine, don't hesitate to ask the staff of your chosen wine shop (or 'cave', meaning cellar) for advice – enjoying a good bottle of wine that complements the food it is served with is seen as an everyday privilege in France, whatever your budget, and knowing about and appreciating wine does not carry the same connotations of snobbery as it can do in the UK.

While France may be more readily associated with wine-drinking, in fact large swaths of the country have a strong

beer-brewing tradition, and in recent years a revival of interest in craft beer has taken hold in Paris. Make sure you sample some of the artisan-produced beers available in Paris – the Paname Brewing Company in the 19th arrondissement on the Bassin de la Villette is one of the nicest places to sit and sip a beer in the city. The food halls of the big French department stores, Le Bon Marché, Galeries Lafayette and Printemps are a treasure trove of luxury food products and a great source of presents to take home.

And then there are the markets – open air or covered, the principle is the same, top quality fish, meat, vegetables, cheeses, delicatessen counters and often hot food stands of anything from Moroccan to Caribbean to Thai street food. On market streets such as the steep and cobbled rue Mouffetard in the 5th or the lively rue Daguerre in the 14th, food shops have often congregated around the permanent stalls, while on a rainy day, browsing a covered market is a brilliant way to pass the time.

Perfect Pâtisseries

Intricate pâtisseries at Senoble.

Is there a more Parisian sight than the colourful ranks of exquisite chocolate éclairs, strawberry tarts and millefeuille pastries arrayed in the window of a pâtissiers shop? From

Ladurée

Pâtisserie Pain de Sucre

Sugar craft: Parisian macarons, pâtisserie and chocolates.

the classics to the more avant-garde interpretation of this very French skill, the alchemy of baking and the artistry of sugar, you'll find everything within the twenty Parisian arrondissements.

And it's not just about cakes and macarons – the art of the chocolatier from sourcing the cacao beans right through to the end product is one that is taken seriously in France, as the number of chocolatiers and confisiers (chocolate and sweet shops) still in evidence on the streets of Paris attests.

It's a mark of how seriously Parisians take their ever-present bread that bakers battle it out every year to be awarded the accolade of Paris' – or France's – best baguette. And don't miss the seasonal specialities: around Easter time an exuberant selection of chocolate Easter eggs, rabbits and fish (yes, Easter calls for chocolate fish in France) are on display in the windows while in January, Epiphany, calls for the buttery galette des rois, on sale in nearly every bakery.

Cosmopolitan Paris

With a colonial history as turbulent as France's, it's hardly surprising that influences from across the globe have found their way into 'French' cuisine across the centuries. The strong identity associated with traditional French cooking – and the sheer variety available within the country's different regions – means that French-born restaurateurs themselves have been slower to adopt the anything-goes borrowing of ideas and flavours from other food cultures that has become the norm in Britain, although this has started to change recently – with innovative chefs melding the fragrances and flavours of far away with traditional French ingredients.

However, thanks to significant waves of immigration into France following conflicts in the former French colonies or, depending on the country, simply thanks to French immigration policies that have allowed large populations to become established, great traditional restaurants serving up the best of Lao or Cambodian, Senegalese or Tunisian cuisine have long been a feature of the Parisian food scene. Paris is also the place to check out specialities from France's overseas departments and territories, mainly made up of French Guiana, Caribbean, Atlantic, Pacific and Indian Ocean islands.

After the terrible war in Indochina, immigrants from the former French colonies that are now Vietnam, Laos and Cambodia brought fragrant soups and crunchy 'nem' rolls to France, with a huge concentration of good options especially to be found in the 13th arrondissement, Paris's biggest Asian quarter as well as in Belleville on the border of the 10th and 20th arrondissements.

France's bloody history in North Africa is still a sensitive subject politically and sociologically but one thing's for sure,

France has enthusiastically embraced cous cous with spicy merguez with slow-cooked chickpeas and vegetables as one of its national dishes, as much appreciated as steak frites or tartiflette. The plethora of restaurants that grew up to cater to the large numbers of people arriving from Morocco, Tunisia and Algeria from the mid-twentieth century onwards are a much-loved part of Paris's food scene.

In the Goutte d'Or region in north east Paris, just a few minutes' walk from the quintessentially French streets of Montmartre, tiny Senegalese and Malian restaurants serve up spicy peanut mafé and bissap juice to a big West African population – well worth a visit for an entirely different take on the French capital.

The prized reputation of French cuisine in Japan meanwhile, has led to a wave of up-and-coming Japanese chefs setting up in Paris and combining these two wildly diverse culinary traditions to great effect.

1st Arrondissement

IF YOU'RE IN PARIS on holiday you're likely to spend a fair amount of time in the 1st arrondissement, home as it is to the world-renowned galleries of the Louvre, the impeccable landscaping of the Tuileries gardens including the charming Musée de l'Orangerie impressionist gallery and part of the higgledy piggledy Île de la Cité, one of two islands accessed by bridges in the middle of the Seine. This was the heart of the city in medieval times and contains some of the City of Light's oldest buildings, dating back to the Middle Ages. The 1st is the least populated of Paris's arrondissements and it's also probably one of the hardest places to negotiate the tourist traps in search of a good quality restaurant or café. That said, if you know where to look there are plenty of (good) surprises.

Pure Paris

LA DAME DE PIC
20 rue du Louvre, 75001. +33 (0)1 42 60 40 40
**https://www.anne-sophie-pic.com/
content/la-dame-de-pic**

The Parisian outpost of celebrated chef Anne-Sophie Pic's culinary empire is a discreetly decorated haven of good taste – perfect for sampling her precise and imaginative cuisine that makes full use of the extraordinary range of raw ingredients France has to offer.

J-F Mallet

Maison Pic

Le Zimmer. Helen Massy-Beresford

LE ZIMMER

1 place du Châtelet, 75001. +33 (0)1 42 36 74 03
http://www.lezimmer.com

The opulent decoration in this traditional brasserie highlights its history – founded by an Alsatian family in 1896 – and still going strong, it serves up brasserie stalwarts such as snails and foie gras today.

HÔTEL COSTES

239 rue Saint-Honoré, 75001. +33 1 42 44 50 00
www.hotelcostes.com

Hang out with the beautiful people at the restaurant – and its lovely terrace – of this opulent Paris institution.

PIROUETTE

5 rue Mondétour, 75001. +33 (0)1 40 26 47 81
www.restaurantpirouette.com

If it's true that we eat with our eyes as well as our taste buds, Pirouette is a treat for the senses with delicate and colourful plates that showcase top notch ingredients and original flavour combinations – think beets and burrata with duck broth or bergamot madeleines with a white chocolate and

Pirouette. Aimery Chemin / Virginie Garnier

A feast for the eyes at Pirouette. Aimery Chemin / Virginie Garnier

tea ganache and thyme and lemon foam. With main courses at around €30, the €45 three-course menu is a great deal. The carefully chosen wine list is full of organic and natural wines which are gaining in popularity among French consumers.

LE MEURICE
228 rue de Rivoli, 75001. +33 (0)1 44 58 10 55
www.alainducasse-meurice.com

At culinary superstar Alain Ducasses's Michelin-starred restaurant, the opulent décor is inspired by the Château de Versailles – nevertheless the cuisine is the star of the show, with deceptively short descriptions putting the high-quality ingredients in the spotlight. The

Collection Menu, at €380 for three dishes, cheese and dessert is a chance to see what a gastronomic master – and his executive chef Jocelyn Herland – can do.

AU PIED DE COCHON
6 rue Coquillière, 75001. +33 (0)1 40 13 77 00
www.pieddecochon.com

As the name – The Pig's Trotter – suggests, not really one for vegetarians, who might find one or two edible options on the menu (though not among the main courses) but may well have to eat them as their neighbours tuck into stuffed pigs' trotters, Périgord-style (€26.50) or 'Mr Pig's Head' (€28), a 70-year-old recipe. Even one of the

Helen Massy-Beresford

salads, the Saint-Antoine (€17.50), contains grilled pigs' ears. This uber-traditional brasserie near the old central market of Les Halles stays open round the clock and has done since it opened in 1947.

L'ESCARGOT MONTORGUEIL

38 rue de Montorgueil, 75001. +33 (0)1 42 36 83 51

www.escargotmontorgueil.com

The name is a bit of a giveaway but if you're after the quintessentially French dining experience of snails this is the place for you. While snails may be the main event, taking in the grandiose early twentieth century décor, including a ceiling decoration by Georges Clairin originally painted for Sarah Bernhardt, is all part of the experience. The recipe for the classic dish of Burgundy snails (six for €12 rising to thirty-six for €70) in parsley butter dates back to 1832, while for the more adventurous there are snails with foie gras, snails in a curry sauce or snails with Roquefort. For mulluscophobes, there's a full menu of non-snail-based dishes too and even frogs' legs (€16), that other French dining cliché, in fact increasingly hard to find on Parisian menus.

MACÉO

15 rue des Petits Champs, 75001. +33 (0)1 85 15 22 56

www.maceorestaurant.com

Precise and beautifully presented dishes served in an airy atmosphere. The lunch menu at €35 is a good bet.

BAR HEMINGWAY

Ritz Paris, 15 place Vendôme, 75001. +33 (0)1 43 16 33 74

www.ritzparis.com

Head to the Bar Hemingway for arguably the best cocktails you'll ever taste, mixed by Colin Peter Field, the bartender and author who has repeatedly been voted the best bartender in the world. You'll also get a taste of a lost Paris, the Paris of the Jazz Age, the Paris of F. Scott Fitzgerald, Cole Porter and of course the man who gave the bar its name, Ernest Hemingway. Slowly sipping a cocktail as you take in the club-house atmosphere of sepia prints and hunting trophies, is a Parisian experience not to be missed.

Helen Massy-Beresford

Best Bistrots

LA RÉGALADE

106 rue Saint-Honoré, 75001. +33 (0)1 42 21 92 40

www.laregalade.paris

The heir of the bistrot of the same name in the 14th that launched the 'bistronomy' movement well over a decade ago, the team behind this relaxed dining room still prides itself on choosing the best ingredients and cooking them well – sounds simple but its enduring popularity attests to the skills involved.

JUVENILES

47 rue de Richelieu, 75001. +33 (0)1 42 97 46 49

http://www.juvenileswinebar.com

This wine bar, with a great selection by the bottle or the glass, including many wines from outside France, plus an imaginative menu of simple, seasonal dishes, is a Paris institution, and for good reason.

CAFÉ BLANC

10 rue Croix des Petits Champs, 75001. +33 (0)1 42 33 55 85.

http://lecafeblanc.com

A good old-school French bistrot, complete with vintage advertising posters lining the walls, good value for the area and with a reliable menu of French classics and daily specials. Good service and a warm welcome.

WILLI'S WINE BAR

13 rue des Petits Champs, 75001. +33 (0)1 42 61 05 09

www.williswinebar.com

You wouldn't expect a wine bar run by a Brit to take off in Paris, but Willi's, set up in the 1980s, quickly became a local favourite and is still going strong, with carefully selected wines and simple but delicious market-style cuisine. Book if you can or just turn up for a quick lunch at the counter, where you can choose one of the daily specials with a glass of wine for €16.90. The evening menu of three courses for €36 is great value.

Helen Massy-Beresford

CAFÉ KITSUNÉ

51 galerie de Montpensier, 75001. +33 (0)1 42 15 62 31

www.kitsune.fr

For a more affordable way to soak up the beauty of the Palais Royal gardens, try the terrace of this Japanese-inspired coffee shop, part of the Maison Kitsuné fashion brand with its kitsch fox logo and playful designs. Choose from a short list of coffees made from carefully selected beans and a selection of cakes, cookies and shortbread. The boutique is just a few steps away in rue de Richelieu.

L'ABSINTHE

24 place du Marché Saint-Honoré, 75001. +33 (0)1 49 26 90 04

www.restaurantabsinthe.com

Inventive ingredients and a lively atmosphere put this upmarket bistrot on the map. With starters, the likes of marinated scallops and sea bream with crisp buckwheat, at €14 and main courses such as red wine braised pork cheeks with trofie pasta at €25 it's not cheap but it is cheerful and the set menus ranging from €32 to €45 a head are good value for this area. Go on a Friday to try the weekly special of macaroni cheese with lobster.

Al Fresco Paris

RESTAURANT DU PALAIS ROYAL

110 galerie de Valois, 75001. +33 (0)1 40 20 00 27

http://restaurantdupalaisroyal.com

Michelin-starred cuisine in the stunningly peaceful and green setting of the colonnaded Palais Royal gardens.

Helen Massy-Beresford

CAFÉ MARLY

93 rue de Rivoli, 75001. +33 (0)1 49 26 06 60
www.cafe-marly.com

It's hard to imagine a more Parisian
panorama than the one from the
terrace of Café Marly, which sits within
the Louvre buildings. Inevitably, given
the location, prices are high (€16 for a
croque monsieur, around €30 for a more
elaborate main course) and service can
be slow but after a morning of vying for
a glimpse of the Mona Lisa at the Louvre
it's worth a visit for an equally Parisian
but more relaxing view.

Going Green

VÉGÉT'HALLES

41 rue des Bourdonnais, 75001. +33 (0)1
40 41 93 95
http://www.vegethalles.fr/

A wide-ranging menu full of vegetarian
takes on classic dishes, with plenty of
vegan options too. The veggie burger
(€13.10) is the house speciality.

LEMONI CAFÉ

5 rue Hérold, 75001. +33 (0)1 45 08 49 84
www.lemonicafe.fr

There's plenty of vegetarian and gluten-
free choice (as well as meaty and wheaty
options too) at this simple café, all blond
wood and sunny yellow accents. The
Cretan-inspired menu changes daily
according to the vegetables available at
the market. Think green bean, mushroom
and basil risotto or salmon with lemon
and sorrel.

Helen Massy-Beresford

Healthy pâtisseries at Foucade.

FOUCADE

17 rue Duphot, 75001. +33 (0)1 42 36 11 81
https://www.foucadeparis.com

Healthy pâtisseries might sound like an oxymoron but Foucade is living proof that they do exist. Try La Fruitée, an exuberant mango tart made with almond pastry and flavoured with coriander and Cambodian kampot pepper – and dairy-free and gluten-free at just 160 calories.

Pop-Up Paris

CANTINE CALIFORNIA

Place du Marché Saint-Honoré, 75001 on Wednesday and Friday lunchtimes.
www.cantinecalifornia.com

Organic and homemade takes on Californian classics such as burgers (€16) and tacos (3 for €13.50) from this popular food truck. There's now a restaurant too at 46 rue de Turbigo in the 3rd.

Café Culture

LE FUMOIR

6 rue de l'amiral Coligny, 75001. +33 (0)1 42 92 00 24
http://lefumoir.com

Soak in the Parisian atmosphere at this wonderful café/bar near the Louvre. The terrace is perfect on sunny days and there's a menu of inventive takes on French classics too.

LE NEMOURS

2 place Colette, 75001. +33 (0)1 42 61 34 14
www.lenemours.paris

A traditional Parisian café with outside tables on the peaceful place Colette, home to the Comédie-Française theatre. There's a menu of simple French dishes done well and a recent revamp has brought the décor bang up to date while maintaining the old-school charm.

CAFÉ VERLET
256 rue Saint-Honoré, 75001.
Buy the coffee – a selection of around thirty of the best varieties from Africa, Asia and South America and beyond – to brew at home or taste on site at this wonderfully traditional coffee roaster.

BAGUETT'S CAFÉ
33 rue de Richelieu 75001. +33 (0)9 54 83 04 86
https://www.facebook.com/baguettscafe/

Part of the Parisian coffee revolution that has taken hold in recent years, this friendly little place is the ideal post-Louvre pit stop for a fortifying espresso and home-made madeleine or slice of quiche.

LE CAFÉ DES INITIÉS
3 place des Deux Écus, 75001. +33 (0)1 42 33 78 29
A typically Parisian café with a perfect terrace for a sunny day.

Do it Yourself

COMPTOIR DES ABBAYES
23 rue des Petits Champs, 75001.
www.comptoir-des-abbayes.fr

Find tea, honey, biscuits and more all produced in one of France's many monasteries at this quirky shop near the Palais Royal gardens.

LE MARCHÉ SAINT-HONORÉ
Place du Marché Saint-Honoré, 75001
Pick up some fresh produce, cheese or charcuterie at this market held on

Wednesday afternoons and Saturday mornings.

LA CAVE DES TUILERIES
232 rue de Rivoli, 75001. +33 (0)1 71 27 45 00
https://lacavedusenat.com/fr/la-cave-des-tuileries-paris

An astonishing selection of over 500 fine wines from champagne to Bordeaux, Burgundy and beyond awaits you in the magnificent vaulted rooms of this upmarket cave à vin (wine cellar).

LE MARCHÉ SAINT-EUSTACHE – LES HALLES
rue Montmartre, 75001. +33 (0)1 43 24 74 39
Around twenty fruit and veg, cheese, charcuterie and wine stands and more make up this little market, which is open on Thursday afternoons and Sunday mornings.

Perfect Pâtisseries

SENOBLE
11 rue des Petits-Champs, 75001
https://www.senoble.com

Try one of the perfect crispy-shelled macarons or the statuesque île flottante with your cup of tea at this patisserie-

Cheesecakes at Senoble. Helen Massy-Beresford

meets tea salon close to the Palais Royal gardens. There's also a branch on the Île Saint Louis (69 rue Saint-Louis-en-Île, 75004).

PIERRE MARCOLINI

235 rue Saint-Honoré, 75001. +33 (0)1 40 20 07 22
www.eu.marcolini.com

A boutique fit for the king of chocolate – a title that could easily be accorded to the eponymous founder who has made it his mission in life to source the best cocoa beans and transform them into delicate and inventive delicacies. Try the Java (€5.50) – a sleek confection of chocolate biscuit, nougatine, coffee, pistachio, chocolate sabayon and white chocolate mousse. Or put together a selection box of the marvellous truffles for an ideal gift.

SÉBASTIEN GAUDARD

1 rue des Pyramides, 75001. +33 (0)1 71 18 24 70
www.sebastiengaudard.com

Walking through the doors of this pâtisserie/tea salon looking out over the Tuileries gardens is like taking a step back in time – it's not just the décor, though that helps, but the selection of timeless cakes and pastries that hark back to a French pâtisserie tradition that is still thriving. Despite the whiff of nostalgia in the air, there is one major sign of modernity: the €32 brunch. There's another boutique in the 9th at 22 rue des Martyrs.

ANGELINA

226 rue de Rivoli, 75001. +33 (0)1 42 60 82 00
www.angelina-paris.fr

Try the signature pâtisserie, the Mont-Blanc, a frothy confection of meringue, whipped cream and chestnut at this equally legendary tea salon a few steps from the Louvre.

Cosmopolitan Paris

OLIO PANE VINO

44 rue Coquillière, 75001. +33 (0)1 42 33 21 15
https://www.facebook.com/Olio-Pane-Vino-252771239036/

A daily changing menu of simple dishes – bruschetta, pasta and the like – as well as high quality Italian wine, oil and more in the grocery section.

YAM'TCHA

121 rue Saint-Honoré, 75001. +33 (0)1 40 26 08 07
www.yamtcha.com

The much-feted chef Adeline Grattard opened yam'Tcha in 2009, bringing together Hong Kong influences and top notch French ingredients. Such has been its success that in 2015 it moved to bigger premises in the well-heeled rue Saint-Honoré where lucky diners – you'll need to be patient and book far in advance to bag a table – enjoy the subtle blend of flavours and exquisite decorative touches of Grattard's cuisine. Check out the yam'Tcha boutique in the nearby rue Sauval for an exquisite choice of teas

YASUBE

9 rue Sainte-Anne, 75001. +33 (0)1 47 03 96 37

Part of Paris's 'Little Tokyo', the rue Sainte-Anne, runs through the first arrondissement and if you're after a Japanese food fix this is the place to find it. Yasube doesn't look like much from the outside but is considered by many Japanese residents of Paris to be one of the most authentic places in the city to enjoy yakitori skewers cooked as they should be over hot coals, skilfully prepared sashimi, tempura and, if choosing is too difficult, a varied and delicious bento box. Book if you can as it gets crowded.

JANTCHI

6 rue Thérèse, 75001. +33 (0)1 40 15 91 07
http://www.jantchi.com

Bibimbap (rice, vegetables and egg with spicy beef, pork or seafood), warming

Bibimbap at JanTchi. Helen Massy-Beresford

plates of noodles, Korean barbecue – everything you'd expect from a Korean restaurant in a simple setting. The €12-14 lunch time set menu is particularly good value in this upmarket area. Get there early on weekday lunchtimes to avoid the rush.

DJAKARTA BALI

9 rue Vauvilliers, 75001. +33 (0)1 45 08 83 11.
http://www.djakarta-bali.com

A taste of Indonesia in the heart of Paris with a good value three-course lunch menu at €19.50.

NODAIWA

272 rue Saint-Honoré, 75001. +33 (0)1 42 86 03 42
http://www.nodaiwa.com/en/

A slightly niche Japanese restaurant specialising in unagi or grilled eel.

2nd Arrondissement

ON WEEKDAYS, THE 2nd is a business-focused arrondissement, home to the old stock exchange and a cluster of upmarket offices that have spawned a thriving lunch scene where service is quick and workers' demand for a little originality in their lunch break has made for a wide variety of different cuisines and concepts. As you stroll around the tourist sights of central Paris, heading from the Louvre through the Jardin du Palais Royal, past the opulent opera to department store heaven in the shape of Galeries Lafayette and Printemps or on to the Place Vendôme for some more serious window shopping, the 2nd arrondissement offers plenty of places for a pit-stop. Many of its food gems are to be found in the covered shopping arcades that date from the nineteenth century and burrow between the district's main streets, providing a welcome break from the Paris drizzle on a rainy day.

Pure Paris

LE MESTURET

77 rue de Richelieu, 75002. +33 (0)1 42 97 40 68.

www.lemesturet.com

A period of fasting is advisable before a trip to Le Mesturet – or at the very least a long and energetic tramp around the galleries of the nearby Louvre. You'll find original takes on French classics – all homemade – at this upmarket, buzzing bistrot, like wild boar bourguignon (€18.50) or salmon fillet served with choucroute and horseradish (€19.90) and an extensive wine list favouring small producers. Desserts (around €9) are absolutely vast – the menu even warns diners with small appetites to steer clear

Julien Mivielle

of the traditional praline-filled pastry the Paris-Brest. But they're delicious, especially the bourbon vanilla crème caramel served with orange-infused shortbread.

AUX LYONNAIS

32 rue Saint-Marc, 75002. +33 (0)1 58 00 22 06
www.auxlyonnais.com

A taste of Lyon's traditional cuisine and a taste of a traditional 'bouchon lyonnais' or Lyonnais bistrot too, in the time-warp zinc, old-wood and tile décor. France's second city and the surrounding mountainous region is known for having

Pierre Monetta

some of the country's richest and most indulgent cuisine: brioche sausage with pistachio, quenelles, suckling pig, foie gras – Paris's veggie revolution has passed this place by but as you would expect from a venue owned by Alain Ducasse the cooking is exemplary. Try the two course lunch menu at €28.

LE GRAND COLBERT

2 rue Vivienne, 75002, 01 42 86 87 88.
www.legrandcolbert.fr

Restaurants don't get much more Parisian than Le Grand Colbert, a majestic space of mosaic tiles, brass railings, soaring pillars and sumptuous velvet curtains. The menu is full of brasserie classics – Burgundy snails,

Le Grand Colbert. Helen Massy-Beresford

oysters, skate wings with capers, beef entrecôte, with many main courses around the €25 mark. It's worth saving room for dessert, not only because they are delicious, but for the fabulously old-fashioned concept of having a groaning dessert trolley wheeled over to your table for you to make your choice. Be warned, the café gourmand (€13.50), often a lighter choice than a real dessert, translates here into a huge array of miniature sweet treats, the likes of mini-crème brûlée, mini-macaron, fruit salad, meringue, profiterole, crème caramel ... easily enough for two.

LE MODERNE
40 rue Notre Dame des Victoires, 75002. +33 (0)1 85 15 23 97.
www.le-moderne.fr
Original takes on classic French dishes, artfully presented in an elegant setting.

Julien Mivielle

Best Bistrots

FRENCHIE
5 rue du Nil, 75002. +33 (0)1 40 39 96 19.
www.frenchie-restaurant.com
This neo-bistrot gets its name from the nickname given to its founder, Greg Marchand, when he worked in Jamie Oliver's Fifteen restaurant in London. As you would expect, fresh, quality ingredients are the priority – cooked with style and originality. There's a €48 menu at lunchtime of four courses and €78 or €128 with paired wines in the evening. There's also a Frenchie wine bar and at number 9, fast-food-style takeaway bites at Frenchie To Go.

HABEMUS
13 rue Monsigny, 75002. +33 (0)1 47 42 92 35
www.habemus-restaurant.fr
High-quality bistrot cuisine, friendly service and a weekend brunch.

UN JOUR À PEYRASSOL
13 rue Vivienne, 75002. +33 (0)1 42 60 12 92
www.unjourapeyrassol.com
Soak up some Provençal sunshine at this restaurant, which specializes in truffles when they're in season, even if outside Paris is grey. You can also stock up with south-eastern French specialities and wine from the Domaine de Peyrassol.

DÉPÔT LÉGAL
6 rue des Petits Champs, 75002. +33 (0)1 42 61 67 07
www.depotlegalparis.com
Éclair-maker par excellence

Christophe Adam (see Chapter 7, 4th arrondissement) is behind this cool all-day venue. Come for top-notch viennoiseries, waffles and smoothies at breakfast time, light lunches of burrata or ceviche, tea-time éclairs of course and cocktails and tapas on the menu in the evening.

LE PAS SAGE
1 passage du Grand Cerf, 75002. +33 (0)1 40 28 45 60

The high-ceilings and eclectic décor give this place an elegant, old-world vibe that fits perfectly with the shopping arcade in which it is located. Inside, the menu of small plates blends old-school French with neo-bistrot imagination with flair. There's also a cosy wine bar next door at number 4.

Al Fresco Paris

LA GRILLE MONTORGUEIL
50 rue Montorgueil, 75002. +33 (0)1 42 33 21 21
http://www.lagrillemontorgueil.fr

The terrace at this home of French staples such as pot-au-feu and beef tartare is a lovely place to pass a summer evening.

DROUANT
16-18 rue Gaillon, 75002. +33 (0)1 42 65 15 16
http://www.drouant.com

There's a decent terrace, protected from the street by a bamboo hedge, at this rather formal but excellent restaurant, which offers a three course weekday lunch menu at €45.

Going Green

NOGLU
16 passage des Panoramas, 75002. +33 (0)1 40 26 41 24
www.noglu.fr

In the land of the baguette ... and the croissant ... and the pain au chocolat, finding gluten-free options isn't always easy, but Noglu is a good one, where you'll be able to choose from a short but tasty menu of gluten-free soups, salads, quiches, burgers and main dishes. The lunch formule at €24 for a soup, quiche and dessert is a great deal – the pastries are the stuff of gluten-free pâtisserie-lovers' dreams, as pretty as they are delicious. Everything on the menu is sans gluten but dairy-free and vegan options are available too. There's another branch in the 7th at 69 rue de Grenelle.

JANINE LOVES SUNDAY
49 rue Montmartre, 75002. +33 (0)1 40 26 56 80
https://www.facebook.com/brasserie2emeartparis

All the atmosphere of a traditional Parisian brasserie – but vegan. Try the vegan pizza, especially.

LA GRILLE MONTORGUEIL

Helen Massy-Beresford

Pop-Up Paris

SUR UN ARBRE PERCHÉ
1 rue du Quatre-Septembre, 75002. +33 (0)1 42 96 97 01
www.surunarbreperche.com

If you've ever dreamed of eating dinner while sitting on a swing, or inside a cosy little cabin, or with a 15-minute shiatsu session between courses – and who hasn't? – this is the place for you. Eccentricity aside, the cooking is imaginative and well-executed: try the weekday three-course menu at €34, with the likes of foie gras with oyster mushroom chutney followed by cod roasted with lemongrass and a dessert of Nutella Paris-Brest.

LA PASCADE
14 rue Daunou, 75002. +33 (0)1 42 60 11 00
www.lapascade.com

It's probably sacrilege to say so, but a pascade, a type of pancake from the Aveyron region of southern France, is somewhere between a crêpe and a Yorkshire pudding. Pascades are the main event at this concept restaurant, with sophisticated savoury versions filled with the likes of scallops, leek, daikon, radish, lemon and truffle oil at €26 or sweet incarnations: try caramelised apple, cream, blueberries and vanilla at €12.

COJEAN
121 rue Réaumur, 75002 and branches all over Paris. +33 (0)1 42 36 46 43
https://www.cojean.fr

Part of a high-quality chain serving up

Cojean. Julien Mivielle

fresh and healthy lunches to the local office workers. Think fresh-pressed juices, lentil and pomegranate salad or mango and chia seed pudding.

Café Culture

MATAMATA COFFEE
58 rue d'Argout, 75002. +33 (0)1 71 39 44 58
http://www.matamatacoffee.com

This small and friendly coffee shop offers great coffee (obviously) as well as homemade cakes, cookies and simple lunches.

LE VAUDEVILLE
29 rue Vivienne, 75002. +33 (0)1 40 20 04 62
www.vaudevilleparis.com

This marble-and-mirror clad spot on the corner of the place de la Bourse (the old stock exchange) serves up French stalwarts with style to a business-focused crowd of office workers from nearby banks, the AFP news agency and the antiques and art district at lunchtime, or is a great place to while away an hour with a coffee or a glass of red.

Do It Yourself

MA CAVE FLEURY
177 rue Saint-Denis, 75002. +33 (0)1 40 28 03 39
www.macavefleury.wordpress.com

Head to Ma Cave Fleury where the owner, Morgane Fleury has made it her mission to bring the biodynamic champagnes of her family champagne house, Fleury Père & Fils, to the wider world. Taste the result of the family's pioneering interest in biodynamic wine-growing practices as well as a carefully chosen selection of other top quality wines in a relaxed atmosphere.

LA FERMETTE
86 rue Montorgueil, 75002. +33 (0)1 42 36 70 96
www.la-fermette-paris.com

A mind-bogglingly comprehensive selection of artisan cheeses, as well as high-quality charcuterie and upmarket groceries such as pickles, jams, juices and pâtés.

KODAMA
30 rue Tiquetonne, 75002. +33 (0)1 45 08 83 44
https://www.shop-kodama.com

There's a breathtaking selection of every kind of tea imaginable in this bar/boutique.

Perfect Pâtisseries

MAISON STOHRER
51 rue Montorgueil, 75002. +33 (0)1 42 33 38 20
www.stohrer.fr

The pretty façade of Paris's oldest pâtissier, dating back to 1730, has nothing on the beauty of its pastries. Delicate religieuses au chocolat: choux pastry, chocolate ganache and crème pâtissière confections that take their name from their supposed resemblance to a nun in her habit; wild strawberry tarts and fraisiers (strawberry and cream cakes) are a treat for the eyes as well as the taste buds. The 'puits d'amour' (well of love), a puff pastry base filled with vanilla cream and topped with caramelised sugar has been popular with sweet-toothed Parisians for almost three centuries. And the 'baba au rhum', was invented by the founder Nicolas Stohrer, so the legend goes, to improve a dry brioche served in the Polish court of King Stanislas, where he was working. He added fortified wine and sweetened cream and the King, who was reading One Thousand And One Nights at the time, named the cake the Ali Baba. When the king's daughter married France's King Louis XV, Stohrer moved with her to the court at Versailles, later opening this shop which has been there ever since.

Alexandre Guirkinger

Helen Massy-Beresford

FOU DE PÂTISSERIE

45 rue Montorgueil, 75002. +33 (0)1 40 41 00 61

www.foudepatisserieboutique.fr

This best-of boutique brings together the star pâtisseries of Paris's finest pastry chefs and chocolatiers: Pierre Marcolini's pistachio and caramel bar, Cyril Lignac and Benoît Couvrand's Equinoxe, Pierre Hermé's outlandishly pink Ispahan cake flavoured with rose, raspberry and lychee: they're all here in one colourful display.

Cosmopolitan Paris

37M2

64 rue Sainte-Anne, 75002.
The name is a nod to the tiny spaces Parisians – and their restaurants – occupy. Inside, the space may be small but the bentos (€12.50 including a bubble tea) are generous and good value.

ENTRE 2 RIVES

1 rue de Hanovre, 75002. +33 (0)1 42 66 15 11
http://www.entre2rives.fr

High quality homemade Vietnamese dishes such as zingy bo bun and warming pho soup in this tiny but charming restaurant. Try the banana nems with chocolate sauce for dessert.

DAROCO

6 rue Vivienne, 75002. +33 (0)1 42 21 93 71
www.daroco.fr

Come to Daroco for high quality, original Italian food in a flamboyant atmosphere. The former Jean-Paul Gaultier boutique has been transformed into this cathedral-like restaurant space, all exposed walls, jungly indoor plants and designer light fittings. Refreshingly, the high-fashion vibe doesn't translate into snooty service – the waiting staff, all decked out in stripey Breton tops in a nod to the premises' former occupant, are super-friendly. Choose from a well-thought out menu of Italian wines, starters, primi, secondi and original pizzas, which average around €16, the likes of white pizza with chestnuts, quince and smoked mozzarella or a pumpkin-based pizza with Sicilian sausage and rosemary.

HANG-A-RI

7 rue Louvois, 75002. +33 (0)1 44 50 44 50
A casual little Korean place full of hungry office-workers and homesick Koreans, all enjoying the likes of bibimbap and tofu soup. It gets busy and the space is small but if you can get in it makes a good pit-stop after a morning trekking through the galleries of the Louvre.

3rd Arrondissement

THE 3RD ARRONDISSEMENT contains part of the buzzing Marais district as well as some of Paris's traditional Jewish quarter. The district has historically been home to the city's textiles industry and still houses hundreds of wholesale fashion boutiques as well as little dressmaking workshops and design studios. For tourists, one of the main draws is the magnificent Picasso museum, while wandering the medieval streets peering into minimalist galleries and just-so boutiques is a great way to spend a morning. There's also a fine selection of dining options for the hungry tourist.

Pure Paris

CHEZ JENNY

39 boulevard du Temple, 75003. +33 (0)1 44 54 39 00

www.chez-jenny.com

The dining room at this uber-traditional Alsatian brasserie, lined with wood panelling and red leather banquettes, manages to be both cavernous and cosy – no mean feat. The menu offers typical brasserie fare from seafood platters to onion soup, snails to steak tartare as well as evidence of the strong German influences in Alsatian cooking: try the choucroute Chez Jenny (€27), a vast dish of sauerkraut served with a selection of pork cuts and sausages (or the choucroute de la mer, a slightly lighter version in which the meat is replaced by haddock, salmon, bream and prawns at €29) or the flammeküche, Alsatian pizza-style tarts loaded up with crème fraîche, lardons and onions.

Best Bistrots

L'ESTAMINET

39 rue de Bretagne, 75003. +33 (0)1 42 72 28 12

http://www. lestaminetdesenfantsrouges.com

As you would expect from a little restaurant tucked away in the Marché des Enfants Rouges, the menu is simple and changes frequently and the ingredients are fresh and, where possible, local. The terrace is a lovely spot.

L'AMBASSADE D'AUVERGNE

22 rue du Grenier-Saint-Lazare, 75003. +33 (0)1 42 72 31 22

www.ambassade-auvergne.fr

There's no better place to sample the culinary riches of the Auvergne than this ambassador of rural France, serving up homemade favourites such as creamy aligot potatoes and smoky sausage

Helen Massy-Beresford

since 1966 to Parisians hankering after a taste of rural life and homesick Bougnats (twentieth-century slang for rural escapees, particularly from the Auvergne and surrounding areas). Try a warm salad of Puy lentils to start (€10) and the famous Salers beef steak with aligot and bone marrow (€27). It's best to work up an appetite before coming here as there's also a fine selection of desserts, including Marcillac-poached pear or for the less sweet-toothed a selection of local cheeses including Fourme d'Ambert, a blue cylindrical cows' milk cheese which dates its origins back to Roman times.

BREIZH CAFÉ

109 rue Vieille du Temple, 75003. +33 (0)1 42 72 13 77.
www.breizhcafe.com

Bertrand Larcher, the man behind this growing Breton-themed empire has taken the humble pancake and run with it, inspired by a journey from Brittany to Japan via Paris to turn traditional Breton fare (Breizh means Brittany in the Breton language) into a fusion-food

concept. This is nothing like your local crêperie, all dark wood and doilies, but a sleek space, with an overwhelming selection of ciders (more than sixty, and not just from Brittany) and crêpes and galettes (the savoury buckwheat versions) that go beyond the usual offerings – a galette filled with herring and Saint-Malo potatoes or a crêpe filled with matcha white chocolate mousse and strawberries, all presented with flair. There's another branch in the 6th at 1 rue de l'Odéon as well as locations in Japan.

Al Fresco Paris

CAFÉ CRÈME

4 rue Dupetit Thouars, 75003. +33 (0)1 42 72 04 06
https://www.facebook.com/cafecremeparis03/

A versatile spot to enjoy the sun with

brunch, burgers, coffee and cocktails all to be enjoyed on a terrace with a people-watching view.

CAFÉ DE LA POSTE

124 rue de Turenne, 75003. +33 (0)1 44 78 92 49
https://www.facebook.com/ Lecafedelaposte/

Fresh salad bowls, simple omelettes, pasta and French toast as well as more substantial daily specials such as bœuf bourguignon are all served up with panache at this sister venue to Café Crème, whose sometimes-sunny terrace is equally popular.

CAFÉ SUEDOIS

11 rue Payenne, 75003. +33 (0)1 42 71 99 79
https://www.facebook.com/ lecafesuedois/

Enjoy homemade cinnamon buns and coffee or simple lunch dishes at the café of the Swedish Institute, which occupies the courtyard of a beautiful old hôtel particulier in the Marais.

Voyez-vous Vinciane Lebrun-Verguethen

Going Green

HANK

Hank Pizza: 18 rue des Gravilliers, 75003. +33 (0)9 72 50 33 68
Hank Burger: 50 rue des Archives, 75003. +33 (0)9 72 44 03 99
www.hankrestaurant.com

Two separate restaurants in the 3rd arrondissement – one specialising in homemade organic burgers and one in traditional Italian-style pizza al taglio (by the slice). The twist? Both are entirely vegan: Hank stands for Have A Nice Karma. There's another branch of Hank Burger at 8 rue de Rochechouart in the 9th.

HANK

LE POTAGER DU MARAIS

24 rue Rambuteau, 75003. +33 (0)1 57 40 98 57

www.lepotagerdumarais.fr

The founders of Le Potager du Marais decided to demonstrate that you can still eat well – and enjoy traditional French cooking – without using any animal products. They've taken traditional French techniques and flavours and adapted them, with great results. Try a starter of mushroom pâté (€8) or that perennial favourite on the chalkboards of Parisian bistrots, Auvergne-style salad, this one with smoked tofu, walnuts and vegan cheese (€17). Everything is homemade, vegan of course and organic and gluten-free bread is available on request.

Pop-Up Paris

SAUCETTE

30 rue Beaubourg, 75003. +33 (0) 9 67 89 32 73

www.saucette.fr

A sausage bar you say? Well ... why not? The founders set out to use the current vogue for street food in Paris to revive an often-overlooked part of the French gastronomic tradition, the humble sausage. They use the best cuts of well-sourced meat to produce their own lower-fat and high-quality bangers and selected the best of the rest from producers all over France. Offbeat ingredients such as sesame seeds and fennel add a modern twist to traditional dishes such as sausages with mashed potato and choucroute (sauerkraut).

PONTOCHOUX PARIS

18 rue du Pont aux Choux, 75003. +33 9 86 70 77 00.

A tiny canteen serving up fragrant Japanese curry.

Helen Massy-Beresford

Café Culture

NEIGHBOURS

89 boulevard Beaumarchais, 75003.

www.honor-cafe.com/neighbours

Great coffee and cakes at this tiny trendy café with a little terrace space out front.

LOUSTIC

40 rue Chapon, 75003. +33 (0)9 80 31 07 06

www.cafeloustic.com

Energising veggie bowls, indulgent cakes and of course, wonderful coffee – this café has been so successful in Paris that a new branch is shortly due to open in Marseille.

BOOT CAFÉ

19 rue du Pont aux Choux, 75003. +33 (0)6 26 41 10 66

https://www.facebook.com/bootcafe/

This tiny haven of delicious coffee and cake inhabits a former cobbler's shop, hence the name.

7 AU MARAIS

7 rue des Filles du Calvaire, 75003. +33 (0)1 42 78 99 20

A friendly little café-delicatessen specialising in pastrami, where you can also pick up products to take away.

LA MAISON PLISSON

93 boulevard Beaumarchais, 75003. +33 (0)1 71 18 19 09

http://lamaisonplisson.com

More than just a restaurant, Maison Plisson is also a high-end grocer with a mission to change the way we approach food. The founders set out to bring the best products to their Parisian clientele, sourcing overlooked ingredients and forgotten specialities from responsible artisan producers: part of their aim was to cut food miles. They also set out to reduce food waste and prioritise producers who share their responsible approach to the food chain. Dine in the airy restaurant on the likes of Channel Islands scallops with salsify and shiitake mushrooms (€28) or pumpkin ravioli with celery, preserved lemons, cashew nuts and coriander (€16) or stock up on bread, wine, cheese and deli items for a picnic. No reservations.

JP Baltel

BREIZH CAFÉ EPICERIE

111 rue Vieille du Temple, 75003. +33 (0)1 42 72 13 77

www.breizhcafe.com

Once you've had a taste of Brittany next door, pop into this high-class grocery store, where producers are carefully selected for their quality, to stock up on artisanal cider, jams and of course buckwheat flour so you can make your own galettes at home – surprisingly easy.

LE BARAV

10 rue de la Corderie, 75003. +33 (0)1 48 04 57 59

www.lebarav.fr

A great selection of wines and, in the bar close by, a short but tasty menu of the likes of rillettes, truffled croque monsieur, cheese platters and daily changing salads and sandwiches. Once you've tasted a few by the glass you can buy a bottle in the cave, where the helpful and knowledgeable caviste will help you select from over 250 different wines.

LE MARCHÉ DES ENFANTS ROUGES

39 rue de Bretagne, 75003. +33 (0)1 40 11 20 40

https://www.parisinfo.com/ shopping/73876/Marche-couvert-les- Enfants-Rouges

Paris's oldest food market dates back to 1615 and is still a favourite today – fresh fruit and vegetables, including organic choices, the makings of a gourmet picnic with olives and artichokes from the Italian deli and hummus and tabbouleh from the Lebanese stand.

Perfect Pâtisseries

PAIN DE SUCRE

14 rue Rambuteau, 75003. +33 (0)1 45 74 68 92

www.patisseriepaindesucre.com

A stunning selection of classics with a twist: a traditional tarte au citron is jazzed up with almond pastry and lime jelly while a confection of rosemary pastry with rhubarb and raspberry compote and an almond and orange blossom mousse is divine.

Pâtisserie Pain de Sucre

Helen Massy-Beresford

POPELINI

29 rue Debelleyme, 75003. +33 (0)1 44 61 31 44
www.popelini.com

Named after Popelini, Catherine de Medici's personal chef, the inventor of choux pastry, these little choux buns are filled with crème pâtissière and topped with a colourful icing crown. They come in nine permanent flavours – dark chocolate, coffee, Madagascan vanilla, salted butter caramel, lemon, praline, cherry and pistachio, chocolate and passion fruit and rose and raspberry plus seasonal specials. There's another branch at 35 rue de Turenne, also in the 3rd, as well as in the 9th at 44 rue des Martyrs and in the 6th at 71 rue de Seine.

JACQUES GENIN

133 rue de Turenne, 75003. +33 (0)1 45 77 29 01.
www.jacquesgenin.fr

An airy and relaxing space where you can enjoy the classics of French pâtisserie but the real draw here are the outlandishly-flavoured chocolates and caramels: everything from gingerbread to coriander, rosemary to tonka bean.

Cosmopolitan Paris

OKOMUSU

11 rue Charlot, 75003. +33 (0)9 67 40 97 27
https://www.facebook.com/okomusu/

This Japanese restaurant specialises in Okonomiyaki, a type of grilled savoury pancake served with a variety of ingredients originating in Osaka. There are other dishes too such as yaki soba, sautéed noodles with pork, squid or vegetables. Everything is homemade from fresh ingredients and service is friendly and efficient even if the space is, as is so often the case in Paris, a little cramped.

GRAZIE

91 boulevard Beaumarchais, 75003. +33 (0)1 42 78 11 96
www.graziegrazie.fr

The industrial décor lends a trendy vibe but in fact the menu is pretty classic, with authentic Italian dishes like panzanella salad (€11) or the Aurora pizza – tomato, buffalo mozzarella and basil at (€15). The cocktail list is where things get interesting. The Bloody Truffle (€12) mixes up truffle vodka and Russian Standard vodka with tomato juice, pecorino and spicy bitters while the Textura Gimlet is a blend of mandarin marmalade, gin or vodka, fresh lime juice and ginger liqueur.

4rd Arrondissement

THE FOURTH ARRONDISSEMENT is a must-see on any Paris visitor's list, taking in as it does the buzz of the Marais – a crowded but charming mash-up of crooked streets and trendy boutiques, loud gay bars and medieval houses – not to mention the charm of the Île Saint-Louis, the pomp of the magnificent Place des Vosges and the world-renowned architecture without and art within of the Pompidou Centre (more commonly known to Parisians as Beaubourg). The diversity of the district is reflected in its food highlights – don't miss falafels from one of the kosher restaurants gathered around 'the Pletzl', in Paris's historical Jewish quarter for centuries and now, from a food perspective, a melting pot of Jewish cuisine from Eastern Europe, the Middle East and North Africa.

Pure Paris

BOFINGER
5-7 rue de la Bastille, 75004. +33 (0)1 42 72 87 82.
Bofinger may be Paris's oldest brasserie and it has an atmosphere to match, all wood panels and leather banquettes and a classic menu of Alsatian specialities.

CHEZ JULIEN
1 rue du Pont Louis-Philippe, 75004. +33 (0)1 42 78 31 64
www.chezjulien.paris
Try out the terrace of this lovely bistrot on a summer evening, with its view out across the Seine to the Île Saint-Louis. On a chillier day dine inside in the Belle Époque style dining room, all mirrors and gilt, red banquettes and glittering chandeliers. The cuisine is delicate and imaginative and with main courses such as scallops with potato purée and chorizo cream at €31, the €26 two-course weekday lunch menu is a good deal.

LA BRASSERIE DU PIED DE FOUET
3 rue de Birague, 75004. +33 (0) 1 48 87 53 16
http://www.aupieddefouet.fr/
Classic brasserie fare in a classic brasserie setting.

LE CAFÉ FRANÇAIS
1-3 place de la Bastille, 75004. +33 (0)1 40 29 04 02
www.cafe-francais.fr
A chic take on the classic Parisian café overlooking the famous place de la

Le Café Français.

Gaspard de la Nuit

Gaspard de la Nuit.

Bastille with a full brasserie-style menu as well as lighter bites.

Best Bistrots

LE TRUMILOU

84 quai de l'Hôtel de Ville, 75004. +33 (0)1 42 77 63 98

www.letrumilou.fr

Traditional French food in a traditional and friendly setting: think eggs mayonnaise, terrine or the supremely pungent andouillette sausage.

GASPARD DE LA NUIT

6 rue des Tournelles, 75004. +33 (0)1 42 77 90 53

www.legaspard.fr

This is a fairly formal take on bistrot cuisine in terms of atmosphere. On weekdays, for €32 you can choose two courses and a glass of wine, choosing from bistrot stalwarts with a modern

touch, such as confit de canard (duck confit) and rabbit with mustard.

LE CAFÉ LIVRES

10 rue Saint-Martin, 75004. +33 (0)1 42 72 18 13

https://www.facebook.com/cafelivresparis/

Choose from a short menu of simple but well executed dishes in a cosy space surrounded by books at this off-beat café in the Marais.

AU PETIT FER À CHEVAL

30 rue Vieille du Temple, 75004. +33 (0)1 42 72 47 47

This tiny bistrot dominated by a traditional zinc bar has a tiny restaurant space at the back and is a taste of Paris past. Choose from wines by the glass and a short selection of simple but delicious dishes – steak tartare, confit de canard, charcuterie platters.

LES FOUS DE L'ÎLE

33 rue des Deux Ponts, 75004. +33 (0)1 43 25 76 67

www.lesfousdelile.com

Choose from simple but impeccably served lunch choices (€26 for three courses) or a more elaborate lunch or evening menu (€33 for three courses) at this lively brasserie on the Île Saint-Louis.

BISTROT DE L'OULETTE

38 rue des Tournelles, 75004. +33 (0)1 42 71 43 33

www.l-oulette.com

Chef Sylvain Tracard brings a taste of the south-west – think foie gras and homemade cassoulet (a rich dish of white beans, sausage and duck from the area around Toulouse) – to this classic bistrot. But there are lighter options too.

Al Fresco Paris

BERTHILLON

29-31 rue Saint-Louis en L'Île, 75004.

www.berthillon.fr

No trip to Paris is complete without a Berthillon ice cream, made with high-quality ingredients and with a selection of enticing flavours, everything from classic vanilla to the likes of gianduja and orange ice cream or Mirabelle plum and Poilâne granola sorbet. Many cafés on the Île Saint-Louis sell it, but the Berthillon shop itself provides the best choice of flavours – they change regularly but if raspberry and rose is on offer, don't miss it. Take your ice cream

to the banks of the Seine and enjoy it while watching the tourist Batobus boats pass by.

LE GRAND CŒUR

41 rue du Temple, 75004. +33 (0)1 58 28 18 90

www.grandcœur.paris

The stripped back interior gives a modern feel to this brasserie but the real magic happens outside. At a crisply dressed table on the terrace you'll be able to enjoy a mix of brasserie stalwarts and more imaginative platefuls, but especially this little haven of peace in the busy Marais.

Going Green

CAFÉ GINGER

9 rue Jacques Cœur, 75004. +33 (0)1 42 72 43 83

www.cafe-ginger.fr

Savoury tarts, soups and salads as well as the homemade desserts – are all vegan at this friendly little place where the buzz words are organic, fresh and healthy, while there's always at least one gluten-free option on the menu.

LE GRAND APPETIT

9 rue de la Cerisiaie, 75004. +33 (0)1 40 27 04 95

www.legrandappetit.fr

While plenty of new kids have arrived on the block in the past decade, Le Grand Appetit has been serving up fresh and healthy vegan and macrobiotic dishes to

4TH ARRONDISSEMENT | 71

health-conscious Parisians since 1986. There's a strong Japanese influence to the ingredients which make up your macrobiotic platter – think homemade pickles, miso and seaweed.

EAT GLUTEN FREE
5 rue Caron, 75004. +33 (0)1 44 61 76 72

The place to stock up on gluten-free goods – and the pizza to take away is a highlight.

Pop-Up Paris

ARTEFACT
23 rue des Blancs-Manteaux, 75004.
www.artefact-marais.com

This unusual space combines an art space devoted to temporary exhibitions by up-and-coming artists, a deli section and some of the best speciality teas and accessories sourced from all over the world.

DANS LE NOIR
51 (restaurant) and 40 (boutique/ tastings) rue Quincampoix 75004. +33 (0)1 42 77 98 04.
www.paris.danslenoir.com

A must-try-once experience in which you dine in the dark, assisted by guides, giving a whole new sensory perspective on what you're eating.
Reservation is essential.

THE GRILLED CHEESE FACTORY
9 rue Jacques Cœur, 75004. +33 (0)1 77 10 67 83
https://www.thegrilledcheesefactory.fr

Few things are more French than bread

and cheese but it's hard to imagine a less French way to combine them. Nevertheless, these all-American grilled cheese sandwiches, whether embellished with bacon, salmon, mac & cheese, pastrami or tuna, are a guilty pleasure that Paris has taken to heart. There's another branch in Montmartre (18th) at 46 rue d'Orsel.

Café Culture

LE PELOTON
17 rue du Pont Louis-Philippe, 75004. +33 (0)6 24 58 02 15
www.bikeabouttours.com

Although this coffee shop doubles as the office for Bike About Tours you don't actually have to book a bike tour to enjoy one of their delicious coffees.

LA CAFÉOTHÈQUE
52 rue de l'Hôtel de Ville, 75004. +33 (0)1 53 01 83 84
www.lacafeotheque.com

Just the place for serious coffee connoisseurs – there are beans from all over the world all telling a different story as well as workshops, tastings and concerts.

Do it Yourself

MAMY THÉRÈSE
19 rue Saint-Antoine, 75004. +33 (0)6 40 17 73 25
http://www.mamytherese.com

As well as the signature madeleines this boutique is famous for, and a well stocked selection of jams and other deli goods, you can buy honey collected from hives located on Paris rooftops – part of a broader trend as Parisians increasingly look towards urban agriculture – and apiculture – to turn their city green and cut down on food miles.

TERRES DE CAFÉ

40 rue des Blancs-Manteaux, 75004. **www.terresdecafe.com**

Everything you need for a top quality coffee, from the beans to the machines – Terres de Café prides itself on carefully sourcing and selecting speciality beans and grinding small amounts of them daily. A coffee subscription makes a great gift.

À LA VILLE DE RODEZ

22 rue Vieille du Temple, 75004. +33 (0)1 48 87 79 36

Founded in 1920, this charmingly traditional grocery store has been supplying Parisians and exiles from the south, the Aveyron to be precise, with tomme fraîche cheese, myriad varieties of sausage and much more ever since.

COMME À LISBONNE,

37 rue du Roi de Sicile, 75004. +33 (0)7 61 23 42 30. **www.commealisbonne.com**

As the name suggests, this is a Portuguese-run place gaining a stellar reputation for its delicious Portuguese coffee and even more delicious pasteis de nata custard tarts. They're so popular

Comme à Lisbonne

you can reserve them online. Tasca, Comme à Lisbonne's sister bistrot/food shop is on the same site and there's another branch in the 9th at 20 rue de Mogador.

LA CUISINE PARIS

80 quai de l'Hôtel de Ville, 75004. +33 (0)1 40 51 78 18 **https://lacuisineparis.com**

English speaking cookery courses on everything from baked goods to bistrot cuisine. Sign up for a market tour followed by a cookery class – a convivial way to get a taste for how many Parisians shop and choose their menus.

Perfect Pâtisseries

L'ÉCLAIR DE GÉNIE

14 rue Pavée, 75004. +33 (0)1 42 77 85 11. **www.leclairdegenie.com**

More works of art than edible treats, the éclairs at master pâtissier Christophe Adam's boutique are almost too good to bite into. Almost. Check out éclair no. 324, a frosted pink confection of rose, lychee and raspberry or no. 309, a

Julien Mivielle

abundance but there's a very modern feel to this boutique, all blonde wood, trailing plants and the trademark fox logo – that extends to the pastries too. Highlights include the dark chocolate tonka éclair (€6), shaped like a sleek gold bullion.

LA BOUTIQUE JAUNE – SACHA FINKELSZTAJN
27 rue des Rosiers, 75004. +33 (0)1 42 72 78 91
www.laboutiquejaune.fr

What 'the yellow shop', with its canary-coloured shopfront, lacks in originality when it comes to choosing its name, it makes up in the sheer variety and quality of Eastern European specialities

splendid lemon-yuzu-meringue mash-up (€6 each). There are numerous boutiques across Paris.

PÂTISSERIE MICHALAK
16 rue de la Verrerie, 75004. +33 (0)1 40 27 90 13
www.christophemichalak.com

Master pâtissier Christophe Michalak's patisseries combine flavour with a playful touch – sweet burger anyone? (It's a crunchy vanilla, sesame and chocolate affair). Or try the fluorescently beautiful lime-yuzu crumble tart. If you fancy yourself following in this TV star's footsteps, book onto one of the three-hour masterclasses on everything from unusual flavour combinations to macarons to praline desserts.

YANN COUVREUR
23bis rue des Rosiers, 75004.
www.yanncouvreur.com

The skills and techniques of classic French pâtisserie are all here in

arrayed within. This Paris institution has been supplying the city with poppy seed strudels, baked cheesecake and challah bread for decades: it opened in 1946. As well as the tempting array of baked goods there's a deli counter packed full of specialities such as pickles, fish roe and herring from Poland, Austria, Hungary and Russia among others.

MIZNON
22 rue des Écouffes, 75004. +33 (0)1 42 74 83 58

Mizon, the street food brainchild of Israeli star chef Eyal Shani, would be equally at home in the Pop-Up Paris section. Small bites of intensely flavourful mezze-style food are all complemented by out-of-this-world fluffy pitta, justifying the perennial crowds. Don't miss the roast cauliflower, the slow-cooked ratatouille, the mint-and-coriander-spiked lamb kebabs ... actually, just don't miss any of it. A new branch has recently opened at 37 quai de Valmy near the Canal Saint-Martin in the 10th.

L'AS DU FALLAFEL
34 rue des Rosiers, 75004. +33 (0)1 48 87 63 60.

The clue is in the name (The Falafel Ace) and connoisseurs say these are the best falafels in Paris – get your sandwich, stuffed to bursting with falafel, hummus, harissa, red cabbage and pickles –to take away or eat at one of the inside tables watching the chefs fry batch after batch of some of the lightest, most fragrant falafels you'll ever taste. Unmissable.

Chez Marianne

CHEZ MARIANNE
2 rue des Hospitalières-Saint-Gervais, 75004. +33 (0)1 42 72 18 86.

Another Marais institution, Chez Marianne, serves up Middle Eastern specialities to a hungry crowd either inside at the canteen-style tables or to take away: long-established Parisian street food. Get a ticket inside before you queue up at the hatch for your takeaway falafel pitta.

8

5th Arrondissement

THERE'S PLENTY TO keep you occupied in the lovely 5th arrondissement, spread out on the Left Bank of the Seine and home to the Latin Quarter, the university district of the city, all honey stone and cobbled streets clustered around the Panthéon, France's great monument to its great men (and a still shockingly small number of women), the Arènes de Lutèce, the remains of a Roman amphitheatre and the Jardin des Plantes (the botanical gardens) which also contains a small zoo and the natural history museum. Not much has changed since Ernest Hemingway described the nearby rue Mouffetard as 'that wonderful narrow crowded market street' in *A Moveable Feast*, a memoir of his years as a struggling writer in Paris – it's still one of the most pleasing streets in the city for a stroll in search of food. After a browse of the permanent market stalls selling fruit and vegetables at the bottom of the street, close to the picturesque fountain and the lovely Saint-Médard church (watch out – the market and most of the shops are completely closed on Mondays and many close on Sunday afternoons too) wend your way up the cobbled hill from bakery to cheese shop to wine merchant picking up provisions.

Pure Paris

LA TOUR D'ARGENT
15 quai de la Tournelle, 75005. +33 (0)1 43 54 23 31
https://tourdargent.com

The history of Michelin-starred La Tour d'Argent, which dates its origins back to 1582, is as intricately woven into the history of Paris as some of its more famous monuments. In recent years its owners have been making efforts to bring Paris's oldest restaurant up to date and recover its lost Michelin stars

Hirama

(it has one now but used to have three) with a new chef, Philippe Labbé, a new menu and the opening of a nearby bakery (2 rue du Cardinal Lemoine). The view from the dining room out across the Seine to Notre Dame cathedral is simply magnificent.

BRASSERIE BALZAR

49 rue des Écoles, 75005. +33 (0)1 43 54 13 67

www.brasseriebalzar.com/

Brasserie Balzar has been serving up choucroute and steaks to the city's intellectuals – it's slap bang in the heart of the Latin Quarter – since 1886.

Best Bistrots

L'INVITÉE

8 rue Thénard, 75005. +33 (0)1 43 54 59 47
www.linvitee.fr

An original take on classic French cuisine in a cool modern setting.

CAFÉ DE LA NOUVELLE MAIRIE

19 rue des Fossés Saint-Jacques, 75005. +33 (0)1 44 07 04 41
https://www.facebook.com/pages/Café-De-La-Nouvelle-Mairie/108280069235531

Great wines by the glass? Check. Chalkboard menu of good value French classics-with-a-twist? Check. A relaxed atmosphere and friendly staff who will help you match them together? Check. The Café de la Nouvelle Mairie has got it all – a lovely place to while away a

few hours and the perfect pit-stop in between the two huge green spaces of the Jardin des Plantes and the Jardin du Luxembourg.

VERSE TOUJOURS

3 avenue des Gobelins, 75005. +33 (0)1 43 31 06 98
www.versetoujours.com

A low-key but high-quality neighbourhood restaurant with friendly English-speaking staff and good value carefully thought out dishes such as salmon and bream with saffron risotto (€15.80) as well as the simpler classics such as roast chicken or steak-frites. From the dessert menu, the nutella tiramisu is popular for a reason.

Al Fresco Paris

CAVE LA BOURGOGNE

144 rue Mouffetard, 75005. +33 (0)1 47 07 82 80

This perfectly located, friendly and casual bistrot serves up French classics: think confit de canard, boeuf bourguignon (naturally) and 'cassolette' the chef's own cassoulet-tartiflette hybrid – a small dish of potatoes and melted cheese, served with a side salad. All accompanied by a glass of burgundy – what else? The setting is perfect – grab a table on the terrace if you can and look out over the cobbled rue Mouffetard stretching up the hill beyond the lovely little fountain and the Église Saint-Médard, the market

La Grande Mosquée de Paris.

stalls and, at the weekends, often an accordion player and a few dancing couples.

LE RESTAURANT DE LA GRANDE MOSQUÉE DE PARIS

39 rue Geoffroy-Saint-Hilaire, 75005. +33 (0)1 43 31 14 32
www.mosqueedeparis.net

Sit down in the shady courtyard of the green-and-white-tiled mosque, built in the 1920s, sip a mint tea and nibble on a

Courtyard of the Grande Mosquée.

sweet pastry. For those in need of even more relaxation the mosque's hammam is open to the public too.

LE SALON DU PANTHÉON

13 rue Victor Cousin, 75005. +33 (0)1 56 24 88 80

http://www.whynotproductions.fr/pantheon/

On top of one of France's oldest cinemas you'll find an elegant salon decorated by one of the greats of French cinema, Catherine Deneuve, serving drinks and light meals – as well as a knock-out little rooftop terrace.

Going Green

VEGAN FOLIE'S

53 rue Mouffetard, 75005. +33 (0)1 43 37 21 89

www.veganfolies.fr

The kind of place that would have been a rarity in Paris even a decade ago is now occupying a prime spot, offering a good selection of vegan and gluten-free savoury offerings such as quiches, lasagnes, salads and sandwiches as well as sweet treats including cupcakes, cookies, tiramisù and vegan cheesecake. Limited seating options so opt for a take away that you could eat in the pretty little Square Médard at the bottom of the hill by the church, or in the Jardin des Plantes, a little further on towards the river.

LE GRENIER DE NÔTRE DAME

18 rue de la Bûcherie, 75005. +33 (0)1 43 29 98 29

www.legrenierdenotredame.fr

Tuck into inventive salads and quiches as well as generous and varied main dishes, like the macrobiotic platter (€18.90) full of rice, seasonal veggies, smoked tempeh, azuki beans and wakamé at this haven for Parisian vegetarians and vegans since 1978. Vegetarian and vegan diets – not to mention sourcing produce from high-quality often organic local producers – may be on the rise now but this cosy little restaurant has been doing it all along.

Pop-Up Paris

COCO DE MER

34 boulevard Saint-Marcel, 75005. + 33 (0)6 20 26 77 67

www.cocodemer.fr

Sample the likes of ceviche (€12), spicy sausage with sweet potatoes (€9) red snapper (€17) or prawn, mango and avocado salad (€12) at this modestly priced Seychelles-themed restaurant where the island vibe is taken as far as a sand-covered floor.

LE BONBON AU PALAIS

19 rue Monge, 75005. +33 (0)1 78 56 15 72

www.bonbonsaupalais.fr

This quirky little sweet shop is every child's – and grown-up child's – daydream. Pastel-coloured marshmallows in tall glass jars vie for space with pralines, liquorice, stripy boiled sweets and rainbow-hued sugared almonds, all made by high-quality French producers bringing together classic sweets and regional specialities like almond-flavoured calissons from Aix-en-Provence.

Café Culture

AU THÉ GOURMAND

14 rue Descartes, 75005. +33 (0)9 50 82 76 70

www.authegourmand.fr

A cosy and friendly tea salon also offering homemade soups and quiches. The cakes and cookies are the stars of the show though, delicious and different: a pretty pastel-toned mojito tart with lime mousse, mint meringues and rum marshmallows, or a gluten-free trio of chocolate mousses on a praline base.

STRADA

24 rue Monge, 75005. +33 (0)9 83 67 83 64
www.stradacafefrance.fr

Strada is part of Paris' coffee revolution. Great coffee – both single origin and blends – and simple but tasty brunch-style food as well as English-speaking staff. What more do you need? There's another branch in the third arrondissement at 94 rue du Temple. Nomad workers on laptops can dominate on weekdays but the no laptop rule at weekends lightens the atmosphere.

CAFÉ SHAKESPEARE & COMPANY

37 rue de la Bûcherie, 75005.
www.shakespeareandcompany.com

The legendary Parisian English-language bookshop, with its creaking staircases and groaning shelves full of literary treasures has added flat whites and cappuccinos to its first editions and folios, opening this welcoming café on its Left Bank site in 2015. Café Lomi coffee, bagels, scones and crumble from Bob's Bake Shop, second-hand books to leaf through or a stunning view through the large windows onto Notre Dame beyond.

CAFÉ LÉA

5 rue Claude Bernard, 75005. +33 (0)1 43 31 46 30

Fun and friendly neighbourhood café with a good choice of simple food too.

Do it Yourself

BREWBERRY

11 and 18 rue du Pot-de-Fer, 75005. +33 (0)1 45 31 12 28
www.brewberry.fr

More than 450 beers from all over the world are on offer in this tiny bar and shop just off the rue Mouffetard. Try them on site accompanied by cheese or charcuterie platters as the friendly owner shares some of her encyclopaedic knowledge of all things beer with you.

ANDROUET

134 rue Mouffetard, 75005. +33 (0)1 45 87 85 05

www.androuet.com

Possibly Paris's best cheesemonger – and that's not a claim to be made lightly in a country where cheese is taken seriously (President Charles de Gaulle once lamented that it was impossible to govern a country with 246 different varieties of cheese.) Most of those 246 seem to be on display on the shelves at Androuet. Well, perhaps not, but it's nonetheless a dizzying array of ash-covered goats' cheeses, huge hunks of comté of different ages and therefore intensities, oozing cows' milk rounds – cheeses of all shapes and sizes from every corner of France and beyond. Take your time and take advantage of the expertise in this temple to cheese. The staff will guide you through your selection, offering little tastes of this and that and explaining the differences in flavour. Depending on the season and therefore the lushness of the grass the cow was grazing on you might be able to taste the different between two different ages of the same tomme de montagne, for example.

GOLOSINO

4 square Vermenouze, 75005. +33 (0)1 45 35 93 80.

https://golosino.fr/mouffetard/

Outstanding authentic pizza, pasta and parmigiana to take away.

Androuet

LES BELLES ENVIES

3 rue Monge, 75005. +33 (0)1 42 38 01 41
www.lesbellesenvies.com

If you're avoiding sugar, Paris can seem
an unwelcoming place, with its shop
windows full of forbidden pâtisserie
delights. Let sugar-free pâtisserie
Les Belles Envies come to the rescue;
they may have ditched the sugar but
they certainly haven't abandoned
the traditional French aesthetics. The
passion fruit tart (€5.50) is a beautiful
circle of passion fruit crème brûlée and
crunchy pastry topped with little puffs of
white chocolate ganache – a treat for the
eyes too. All Les Belles Envies' products
are marked with a glycaemic index score
so you can tell how much your sweet
treat is going to raise your blood sugar
level in advance. There's another branch
at 17 rue Poncelet in the 17th.

CARL MARLETTI

51 rue Censier, 75005. +33 (0)1 43 31 68 12
www.carlmarletti.com

The éclairs and tarts on display in this little
shop near the rue Mouffetard are exquisite
feats of engineering. If your French is up to
it you can learn from the sugar master at
one of his thematic masterclass workshops
– details on the website.

Les Belles Envies

LA MAISON DES TARTES

67 rue Mouffetard, 75005. +33 (0)1 45 35 53 90

A fine selection of sweet tarts and savoury quiches to eat in or take away.

ÉRIC KAYSER

14 rue Monge, 75005. +33 (0)1 44 07 17 81 **www.maison-kayser.com**

This legendary baker is famous primarily for the wonderful selection of artisanal breads – sourdough, rye, with olives, dried fruits or cheese, there's something for everyone. The cakes and pastries are divine too – try the madeleine: plain, chocolate, pistachio or raspberry. In a sign of the times, there's even a gluten-free range. This is the original branch but there are now outposts all over Paris and beyond.

Cosmopolitan Paris

GODJO

8 rue de l'École Polytechnique, 75005. +33 (0)1 40 46 82 21

Varied and vibrant curries are served on vast sharing platters to be mopped up with the traditional injera buckwheat pancakes (no cutlery needed) at this friendly and relaxed Ethiopian restaurant in the heart of Paris's student quarter. The selection of meat and vegetable dishes at €19 or the vegetarian version at €16 – are a good option if you haven't eaten Ethiopian food before and want a taste of everything and a balanced set of flavours.

LE LHASSA

13 rue de la Montagne Sainte Geneviève, 75005. +33 (0)1 43 26 22 19

It's not everyday you get to try Tibetan food but at this cosy little restaurant dishes like barley and spinach soup, momos (Tibetan dumplings), spicy potato curry and grilled beef come with a side order of friendly service too. There's plenty of choice for vegetarians. Just watch out for the traditional Tibetan tea made with yak's milk ... an acquired taste.

9

6th Arrondissement

THE 6TH IS ONE of Paris's most expensive arrondissements to live in and it shows – narrow little streets lined with upmarket fashion boutiques and pared-back art galleries. It boasts some of the prettiest views in Paris, from the manicured gardens of the Jardin du Luxembourg, which also houses the French senate building and is a lovely place to while away a sunny day, to the magnificent Seine vistas from the padlock-littered Pont des Arts and the pleasing lines of the Saint-Sulpice church. The world-famous boulevard Saint-Germain used to be the heart of Paris's intellectual life: Jean-Paul Sartre and Simone de Beauvoir discussed existentialism at the Café de Flore while Pablo Picasso and Ernest Hemingway were once regulars at Les Deux Magots. Now the boulevard is dominated by haute couture, and these last surviving literary haunts and the few remaining bookshops can only hint at the area's glorious past.

Pure Paris

RESTAURANT GUY SAVOY
11 quai de Conti, 75006. +33 (0)1 43 80 40 61
www.guysavoy.com

Considered by many to be Paris's best restaurant – although deciding how to set out the criteria to define that category could be a life's work – Guy

Savoy is a true taste of haute cuisine, French-style. It's not just the precision of the flavours in classic dishes such as whole-roasted red mullet served with mushrooms, green beans and baby squid, dressed with a jus of red mullet liver or for dessert, millefeuille with Tahitian vanilla cream whipped up by the restaurant's expert pastry chef. It's also

La Monnaie de Paris – the Paris Mint, which also houses Guy Savoy's eponymous restaurant Laurence Mouton

Lobster at Guy Savoy. Laurence Mouton

the exquisitely engineered presentation, the discreetly luxurious attentions of the sommelier and waiting staff and

Chocolate money, Guy Savoy-style.
Laurence Mouton

of course the breath-taking views of the Seine. None of this comes cheap, of course – the Colours, Textures and Flavours menu is about €450 without drinks. The restaurant reserves one lunch table each day for would-be gastronomes hesitating about whether to try the restaurant. If you can book ahead and be prepared to arrive at 12 p.m., you'll have the choice of a starter, main course and dessert for €130 with wine by the glass starting at €10.

LE PROCOPE
13 rue de l'Ancienne Comédie, 75006. +33 (0)1 40 46 79 00
www.procope.com

This mythic restaurant has been around since 1686, serving Diderot and Rousseau among many other emblematic French figures over the centuries. Today its specialities reflect that history, with calf's head, coq au vin and braised beef cheeks among the favourites, but the fabulous seafood platters offer a fresher plateful too.

BRASSERIE LIPP
151 boulevard Saint-Germain, 75006. +33 (0)1 45 48 53 91
www.brasserielipp.fr
Brasserie classics, perfectly presented in a perfectly Parisian setting.

BOUILLON RACINE
3 rue Racine, 75006. +33 (0)1 44 32 15 60
www.bouillonracine.com
An art nouveau gem – the interior of this 'bouillon' – originally a restaurant that catered to workers in need of a

cheap and cheerful lunch, has a much more sophisticated décor than those origins would suggest. Classics and more modern dishes coexist on the menu which prides itself on its good quality ingredients that show off the best of the French regions.

Best Bistrots

L'AVANT COMPTOIR DU MARCHÉ
14 rue Lobineau, 75006.
https://www.facebook.com/ lavantcomptoir/

Yves Camdeborde, the pioneer of the bistronomy movement that sought to marry a relaxed dining vibe with fine ingredients and skilful cooking, brings the same principles to bear at this lively market bistrot. Order charcuterie-dominated tapas plates to share as you sip (or glug, they're pleasingly chunky

L'Avant Comptoir du Marché. Helen Massy-Beresford

glasses) your way through the ever-changing selection of wines on the chalkboard.

LA LOZÈRE
4 rue Hautefeuille, 75006. +33 (0)1 43 54 26 64
www.lozere-a-paris.jimdo.com

Just across the road from the Lozère tourist office is this low-key but charming restaurant where you'll have the chance to try the regional dishes from this little-known and mountainous region of southern France near the Massif Central. Don't miss the saucisse-aligot available as part of the €23.90 three-course menu – smoky sausage served with creamy 'aligot' mashed potato, a true mountain dish prepared by beating fresh tomme cheese, cream and garlic into mashed potatoes.

CRÊPERIE DU VIEUX JOURNAL
17 rue Bréa, 75006. +33 (0)1 43 26 90 49.

This rather old-fashioned (charmingly so) family-run restaurant is a great place to

Crêperie du Vieux Journal. Helen Massy-Beresford

stop for a reasonably priced meal in this expensive district: service is friendly and the galettes and crêpes are good quality. Try the sweet crêpe with apples flambéed in calvados (€7.50) for dessert. If you're there around Christmas ask the owner to show you the amazing traditional Christmas decorations including an elaborate nativity scene in the back courtyard.

LA CHARETTE CRÉOLE
15 rue Jules Chaplain, 75006. +33 (0)1 43 26 03 10

Spicy specialities from the islands of La Réunion – an overseas department of France in the Indian Ocean – as well as Madagascar and Mauritius. Try the Indian-influenced cabrie massalé (goat curry) from La Réunion or one of the many fish specialities.

LE COMPTOIR DU RELAIS
9 carrefour de l'Odéon, 75006. +33 (0)1 43 29 12 05
http://www.hotel-paris-relais-saint-germain.com/savourez-les-restaurants.html

A very Parisian bistrot with terrace tables and an Art Deco interior, where chef Yves Camdeborde (this is another outpost in his culinary empire), one of the protagonists of the bistronomy movement, serves up imaginative versions of the stalwarts of French cuisine – simpler cooking at lunch time and a more sophisticated set menu in the evenings. You'll need to book.

Al Fresco Paris

LA TABLE DU LUXEMBOURG
Jardin du Luxembourg, 7 rue Guynemer, 75006. +33 (0)1 42 64 88
www.latableduluxembourg.com

Choose from simple sandwiches (ham or comté cheese, €6) or more serious snacks like slow-cooked lamb baguettes (€8) – as well as hot drinks, crêpes, waffles and custard tarts from the takeaway counter. Or choose from a full menu with main courses around (€25) and a gargantuan €50 Sunday brunch in the airy interior.

La Table du Luxembourg. Helen Massy-Beresford

LA CLOSERIE DES LILAS.
171 boulevard du Montparnasse, 75006. +33 (0)1 40 51 34 50
www.closeriedeslilas.fr

Choose between the brasserie menu or more intricate fine dining options as you sit back and enjoy the leafy, jungly terrace.

HUGUETTE BISTRO DE LA MER
81 rue de Seine, 75006. +33 (0)1 43 25 00 28
www.huguette-bistro.com

A wonderful selection of fish and seafood and a charming green and spacious terrace too.

Going Green

HOT VOG
10bis rue Vavin, 75006. +33 (0)1 42 49 36 69

Vegan hot dogs are the main draw here but try the selection of vegan cakes, waffles and other desserts as well as high-end juices. Excellent quality and perfect picnic fare – it's close to the Jardin du Luxembourg if you don't feel like perching in the tiny interior.

Hot Vog. Helen Massy-Beresford

SENSE EAT
39 rue Mazarine, 75006. +33 (0)1 46 34 54 71.
www.senseeat.fr

This is high-end Italian cuisine – it's all vegetarian and there are plenty of options suitable for vegans and those avoiding gluten or lactose too. The menu

is inventive and everything is made from carefully selected organic ingredients sourced from local or Italian producers who respect the environment. Proprietor Enrico Einaudi, himself a vegetarian, was dismayed at the lack of gourmet options for non-meat-eaters and teamed up with renowned chef Maurizio Carlucci to demonstrate that respect for the environment and one's body did not have to equal deprivation. Keeping it in the family, Einaudi's mother makes the fresh pasta (including a gluten-free version). The €19 two-course set menu is a good deal.

PARADIS MARGUERITE
27-29 quai des Grands Augustins, 75006.
+33 (0)1 43 54 51 42
www.paradismarguerite.fr

Easy to spot because of the life-size (fibreglass) cow grazing on the terrace, this airy modern restaurant is a great address for vegetarians as well as carnivores seeking a break from steak frites, pâté and the rest. Choose from an eclectic menu including veggie burgers (€14.50), quinoa salad (€9.50), pizza (€12) and chilli sin carne (€14) – there are plenty of vegan options too and these are clearly marked on the menu.

Pop-Up Paris

FRAPPÉ BY BLOOM
2 rue Guénégaud, 75006. +33 (0)7 89 83 79 58
www.monnaiedeparis.fr

The latest opening by Bloom, a small chain which focuses on fresh healthy ingredients in the form of soups, salads and sandwiches. Here within the old Paris mint, Frappé by Bloom inhabits a gloriously airy and verdant space and serves up veggie-friendly home made dishes, snacks, cakes and smoothies plus a €35 weekend brunch.

COFFEE CLUB
87 rue d'Assas, 75006. +33 (0)1 43 29 87 87
www.coffee-club.fr

This American take on gastronomy has plenty of Parisian fans, piling into the industrial-vibed restaurant for the likes of huevos rancheros (€13.50), fresh-squeezed juices (€6), home-made salads and indulgent desserts such as cheesecake (€8.50).

Helen Massy-Beresford

Café Culture
LE ROSTAND
6 place Edmond Rostand, 75006. +33 (0)1 43 54 61 58

The big draw here is the beautiful location, overlooking the Jardin du Luxembourg: just

the place for a coffee and a spot of people watching. There's a brasserie-style menu of reliable classics too.

CAFÉ DE FLORE
172 boulevard Saint-Germain, 75006. +33 (0)1 45 48 55 26
www.cafedeflore.fr

The haunt of the artists, writers and philosophers of the day through the twentieth century, Café de Flore is a portal to Paris Past. This area, not far from the grandiose buildings of the Latin Quarter and the Sorbonne University, used to be the intellectual heart of the city – it's now more of a high-fashion hub. While you'll find a more exciting menu elsewhere, it's worth a visit to soak up the atmosphere that over a hundred years of serving up glasses of red and little cups of espresso to the city's intelligentsia have lent the space.

LES DEUX MAGOTS
6 place Saint-Germain-des-Prés, 75006. +33 (0)1 45 48 55 25
www.lesdeuxmagots.fr

This famous Paris drinking spot is as much a part of the city's history as Café de Flore. With an espresso at €4.70 you're paying for the legend as much as for the coffee but it's still hard to beat the terrace on a hot summer's day.

LE SELECT
99 boulevard du Montparnasse, 75006. +33 (0)1 45 48 38 24

While it also offers a full menu (try the

Périgord chicken roasted in its own juices at €20.90), coming to people-watch from the pavement tables of Le Select, a hangout for the stars from the 1920s onwards, is a pleasure in its own right.

TREIZE AU JARDIN
5 rue de Medicis, 75006.
www.treizebakeryparis.com

Treize – 13, a baker's dozen – is in a prime spot overlooking the Jardin du Luxembourg, with a charmingly cluttered vintage décor, a non-smoking terrace and friendly staff serving up great coffee, cocktails and American South-inspired breakfasts, brunches and lunches including delicious buttermilk biscuits (similar to scones).

Treize terrace. Helen Massy-Beresford

MARCHÉ SAINT-GERMAIN
4-6 rue Lobineau, 75006.
http://equipement.paris.fr/marche-couvert-saint-germain-5466

This small market nonetheless has a bit of everything: fruit and veg, cheese, fish, wine, deli and grocery items. It's open every day except Monday.

DA ROSA
62 rue de Seine, 75006. +33 (0)1 40 51 00 09
www.darosa.fr

This legendary épicier imports the best of Spain, Portugal and Italy to hungry and discerning Parisians.

LA CRÈMERIE
9 rue des Quatre Vents, 75006. +33 (0)1 43 54 99 30

Enjoy the exquisite small plates and charcuterie boards in this tiny wine bar/épicerie. There's a charming vintage vibe and the walls are lined with edible and drinkable treasures so you can leave with a souvenir.

MAISON BREMOND
8 cour du Commerce Saint-André, 75006.
+33 (0)1 43 26 79 72
www.maison-bremond-1830.com

There's a wonderful selection of gourmet products at this extremely traditional shop (one of several branches across central Paris) – Maison Bremond began life in Aix-en-Provence in 1830 as a manufacturer of calissons, almond-based sweets. It now stocks a wide range of oils and vinegars, speciality salts, spices, biscuits, sweets, jams and more.

Perfect Pâtisseries

PIERRE HERMÉ

72 rue de Bonaparte, 75006. +33 (0)1 43 54 47 77

www.pierreherme.com

Pierre Hermé was voted the world's best pastry chef in 2016 and as you cross the threshold into his temple to the art of sugar, it's easy to see why. The Madame Figaro, from €7.20 for an individual-sized tart, truly looks too good to eat, an orange and raspberry financier, orange blossom brioche topped with crème brûlée, light cream, candied fruit and edible flowers. The sober exterior of the tarte infiniment vanille (€8.30) hides a sweet shortcrust pastry, white chocolate and vanilla ganache, vanilla-moistened biscuit and vanilla-flavoured mascarpone cream, managing, somehow, to stay on the right side of sickly.

ARNAUD LARHER

93 rue de Seine, 75006. +33 (0)1 43 29 38 15.
www.arnaudlarher.com

These are, according to some connoisseurs, the best macarons in Paris and the lemon tart hits just the right note of sweet acidity, but the real draw here is the chocolate – whether you go for pralines, truffles or a simple bar made from cocoa beans specially sourced from Brazil, don't miss out

on one of France's best chocolatiers. There are two other Parisian boutiques in the 18th arrondissement, at 57 rue Damrémont and 53 rue Caulaincourt as well as outlets in Athens and Tokyo too.

Cosmopolitan Paris

CHEZ BÉBERT

71 boulevard du Montparnasse, 75006. +33 (0)1 42 22 55 31

www.restaurantchezbebert.com

This old-fashioned establishment brings together Moroccan cuisine and décor and the traditional French brasserie vibe. Think pastillas, lamb, prune and grilled almond tagine or spicy merguez sausages served with couscous.

HAPPY DAYS DINER

25 rue Francisque Gay, 75006. +33 (0)1 43 29 67 07

www.happydaysdiner.com

Burgers, hot dogs, milkshakes and everything you'd expect from an American diner (as well as some vegan options) with a décor that will have you expecting The Fonz to walk through the door at any moment.

10

7th Arrondissement

AMONG THE CITY'S MOST chic arrondissements, the 7th is home to the French parliament (L'Assemblée nationale) as well as many ministries and embassies. It's hardly surprising then that there is no shortage of upmarket restaurants ideal for business lunches. Finding a more casual and authentic bite to eat is a little more of challenge – but still possible.

The 7th is also full of museums – some highlights are the Musée d'Orsay, a former railway station which is now home to a world-class art collection and the absolutely fascinating Musée du quai Branly with indigenous art from all over the world housed in an original building designed for the purpose. The imposing edifice of the Invalides military museum and monument drips with gilt and embodies the grandiose architecture of this part of the city.

Cross over the Alexandre III bridge to reach the seventh from the north bank and marvel at the ostentatious golden figures. The Esplanade des Invalides beyond is a rare expanse of green in the city centre where you're allowed to walk on the grass and even have a picnic.

The 7th's star attraction is of course the city's most famous landmark, the Eiffel Tower and once you've queued up and climbed it, one of the great pleasures of strolling around this part of Paris is turning a corner and seeing its huge silhouette loom over you when you least expect it.

Pure Paris

LE JULES VERNE/LE 58 TOUR EIFFEL
Avenue Gustave Eiffel, 75007.
https://www.restaurants.toureiffel.com

Much-fêted chefs Thierry Marx and Frédéric Anton have taken over the Eiffel Tower's restaurants, reopening after refurbishment in spring 2019. You can also check out the fresh flavours of Marx's cooking at L'Étoile du Nord, inside the Gare du Nord in the 10th. Or for a special occasion, dive into Anton's

PhotoPoint.Com

luxurious culinary universe at the Pré Catelan in the bois de Boulogne in the 16th.

LE GRAND BISTRO DE BRETEUIL

3 place de Breteuil, 75007. +33 (0)1 45 67 07 27

http://www.legrandbistro.fr

The express lunch menu at this exuberantly-decorated place with a great terrace – €25 for a starter, main course and coffee with a mini dessert – is just the thing after a morning's sight-seeing. Or à la carte, the seafood platters are a speciality.

LES FABLES DE LA FONTAINE

131 rue Saint-Dominique, 75007. +33 (0)1 44 18 37 55

www.lesfablesdelafontaine.net

You'll find a contemporary light-filled setting as the backdrop to fish and seafood specialities at this Michelin-starred establishment. The €28 weekday lunch menu of two courses is excellent value.

LE PERTINENCE

29 rue de l'Exposition, 75007. +33 (0)1 45 55 20 96

https://www.restaurantpertinence.com/en/

A perfect fusion of French cuisine and Japanese techniques in this tiny Michelin-starred spot where the €38 weekday lunch menu is great value.

Best Bistrots

CAFÉ CONSTANT

139 rue Saint-Dominique, 75007. +33 (0)1 47 53 73 34

http://www.maisonconstant.com/cafe-constant/

The various lunch deals offer good value for money in an expensive district: expect fresh and seasonal ingredients transformed into simple dishes such as sea bream with pesto and mushroom risotto or Basque-style veal with white beans. No reservations.

L'AMI JEAN

27 rue Malar, 75007. +33 (0)1 47 05 86 89

www.lamijean.fr

Chef Stéphane Jego, Breton by birth, nevertheless brings a taste of the Basque country – think hearty cuts of pork with spicy twists and don't miss the renowned rice pudding for dessert – to the chic 7th. L'Ami Jean has been a pioneer of the bistronomy movement since it opened in 2004 – in practice that means high quality ingredients transformed by talented chefs into innovative dishes, but crucially all in a casual setting. Try one of the tasting menus. The location makes for a wonderful after-dinner stroll – if you time it right you can watch the nearby Eiffel Tower twinkling away as it lights up on the hour. L'Ami Jean is hugely popular and tiny so be sure to book ahead if you can.

CAFÉ DU MARCHÉ

38 rue Cler, 75007. +33 (0)1 47 05 51 27
Good value for French classics like steak tartare (€14) done well in a friendly atmosphere.

CLOVER

5 rue Perronet, 75007. +33 (0)1 75 50 00 05

http://www.jeanfrancoispiege.com

One of the stars of the world of French gastronomy, Jean-François Piège, is the man behind this inviting modern space, where tasting menus ranging from €37 to €73 will lure you in with the promise of fresh and inventive dishes that showcase the best of French cuisine.

Al Fresco Paris

DIVELLEC

18 rue Fabert, 75007. +33 (0)1 45 51 91 96
http://www.divellec-paris.fr/en/

Precise and imaginative cooking allows the flavours to shine through at this refined seafood and fish place, with a shady terrace perched on the edge of the broad expanse of green that is the Esplanade des Invalides. With starters beginning at around €28 (think clam gratin with thyme and lemon) and main courses such as monkfish, nutmeg, peas and wild asparagus from around €44 the four course discovery menu at €90 is a good deal. Fish are also available to order by weight depending on availability and there's a €49 weekend brunch (€65 with a glass of champagne).

LE BASILIC

2 rue Casimir Périer, 75007. +33 (0)1 44 18 94 64
http://www.restaurant-le-basilic.fr

The menu at this elegant restaurant is pretty classic – chicken supreme with morel sauce, steak tartare – with a few more exotic twists such as fish and chips or Thai-style tuna steak. The setting is the real attraction here though, choose a table on the leafy (heated) terrace looking out onto the quiet little square and the Basilique de Sainte-Clotilde. For an al fresco Parisian meal it's hard to beat.

Café Culture

CUILLIER

68 rue de Grenelle, 75007.

Great coffee and a short but sweet menu of cakes, granola, soup, sandwiches and quiches. Closed at the weekend.

COUTUME

47 rue de Babylone, 75007. +33 (0)1 45 51 50 47.
www.coutumecafe.com

If you're serious about your coffee, don't miss out on a caffeine fix at Coutume. Try one of the single origin espressos – two are available every day – or for filter coffee lovers, Coutume offers V60, Chemex or AeroPress options, all with beans that are carefully selected from growers as far afield as Burundi, Brazil and Laos and then roasted on site in Paris. The original Coutume is in the 7th arrondissement but its little sister opened its doors in the 10th arrondissement (8 rue Martel) in 2017.

Do It Yourself

LA GRANDE ÉPICERIE DE PARIS

38 rue de Sèvres, 75007. +33 (0)1 44 39 80 00
www.lagrandeepicerie.com

The food hall of Le Bon Marché, just up

Bon Marché. Helen Massy-Beresford

the road from the upmarket Parisian department store which claims to be the world's first, is the stuff of gourmet dreams for the sheer variety of luxury goodies from every corner of France and far beyond. Check out luxury items such as truffles, foie gras and caviar, deli counters full of sumptuous ready made dishes and pâtisseries to die for. There's another branch at 80 rue de Passy in the 16th arrondissement.

MARIAGE FRÈRES

56 rue Cler, 75007. +33 (0)1 43 19 18 54
www.mariagefreres.com

This ultra-traditional brand has been supplying tea-savvy Parisians with every kind of tea imaginable (it now stocks over 650 varieties of tea from thirty-six countries) since 1854. The tea salon at the same address as this wonderfully olde-worlde tea-tin-lined shop also offers everything from brunch to lunch to afternoon tea including tea-infused recipes. There are more tea salons and shops across Paris too.

TRUFFES FOLIE

37 rue Malar, 75007. +33 (0)1 44 18 05 41
www.truffesfolies.fr

With everything from truffle pasta to truffle sauce, truffle honey to truffle popcorn (yes really) this is the place for truffle fans. Stock up in the grocery section or stop off at the restaurant for a – you've guessed it – truffle-themed lunch.

Perfect Pâtisseries

HENRI LE ROUX

52 rue Saint-Dominique, 75007. +33 (0)1 82 28 49 84
www.chocolatleroux.com

The son of a celebrated pâtissier, Henri Le Roux studied to be a chocolatier before setting up on his own in Brittany. Wanting to do something a bit different that took inspiration from local food traditions, he came up with salted butter caramel, patenting it in 1981 as CBS (caramel au beurre salé).

Maison Le Roux St-Dominique.
Maison Le Roux - chocolatier & caramélier

Helen Massy-Beresford

Marlon

DEBAUVE & GALLAIS
30 rue des Saint-Pères, 75007. +33 (0)1 45 48 54 67
https://debauve-et-gallais.fr

These are chocolates fit for a queen, literally, despite the fact that France hasn't had one for centuries: founder Sulpice Debauve, the royal physician, originally developed the chocolates that are still sold as 'pistoles de Marie-Antoinette', in the eighteenth century to mix with a headache remedy for the queen. There's another boutique in the 2nd at 33 rue Vivienne.

Cosmopolitan Paris

MARLON
159 rue de Grenelle, 75007. +33 (0)1 40 60 12 12
http://www.restaurantmarlon.fr/

Come to Marlon for laid-back Californian-influenced cuisine in a modern and airy space – choose from main courses of the likes of miso tuna or baby back ribs or lighter options of salads and sandwiches. At the weekends there's an eclectic but broadly American-style brunch menu – you fill in a little form at your table to place your order.

NAGI
121 rue de l'Université, 75007. +33 (0)1 45 56 95 42

Great homemade Lebanese specialities from a talented chef at this friendly and unpretentious place. Choose from hot and cold mezze and grilled meats and don't miss the selection of Lebanese wines. There are a few outside tables for sunny days.

8th Arrondissement

THE WIDE GRANDIOSE boulevards of the 8th arrondissement are typically Parisian – and as well as the presidential palace, this chic district is home to possibly the most famous street in the world, the Avenue des Champs-Élysées, topped by the imposing Arc de Triomphe and coming into its own every year as the 14 July military parade marches down it towards the place de la Concorde.

Hidden among the business-lunch focused restaurants catering to the district's large number of offices and the touristy chain restaurants that line the Champs-Élysées itself, there are some good quality places to eat and drink – if you know where to look.

Pure Paris

LE GRAND RESTAURANT

7 rue d'Aguesseau, 75008. +33 (0)1 53 05 00 00
http://www.jeanfrancoispiege.com

The more formal cousin of Clover, in the 7th, is another chance to sample the imaginative cuisine of gastronomic star Jean-François Piège in an intimate setting (just 25 places). Clover Grill at 6 rue Bailleul and La Poule au Pot at 9 rue Vauvilliers in the old Les Halles market district, both in the 1st arrondissement, are the other members of the family.

LE TAILLEVENT

15 rue Lamennais, 75008. +33 (0)1 44 95 15 01
www.taillevent.com

This Parisian institution, which won its first Michelin star in 1948, is a masterclass in fine dining, from the elegant setting, to the high quality of the seasonal (of course) ingredients, to the precision of the cooking, the theatre of the service – table-side slicing, dicing, flambéing and serving – the choice and quality of wines in the restaurant's cellar and the skill of the wine-and-food pairing. The seven-course 'Quintessence' menu comes in at €198 or the three-course lunch menu at €88.

LES 110 DE TAILLEVENT

195 rue du Faubourg Saint-Honoré, 75008. +33 (0)1 40 74 20 20
http://www.les-110-taillevent-paris.com

One hundred and ten wines by the glass, each glass paired with seasonal dishes to bring out the best in both, offer a more affordable taste of the Taillevent.

APICIUS

20 rue d'Artois, 75008. +33 (0)1 43 80 19 66
http://restaurant-apicius.com

A dream of a location with fine dining to
match, Michelin-starred Apicius is named
after the Roman author of the first ever
cookbook – he would probably approve
of the exuberant menu stuffed with
lobster, frogs' legs, pigs' trotters, calf's
head, pigeon and huge côtes de bœuf.
Tasting menus range from €180 to €220
but as always, prices for à la carte dining
come in much higher.

LE CINQ

31 avenue George V, 75008. +33 (0)1 49 52
71 54

www.restaurant-lecinq.com

Awarded three Michelin stars in 2016,
2017 and 2018, this is Parisian fine-dining
at its best from chef Christian Le Squer,
within the opulent confines of the Four
Seasons Hotel George V. The lunch menu
at €145 for four courses or €210 for six
allows guests the chance to sample the
likes of iced sea urchin soufflé, grilled
cod with black truffle and candied
banana with coffee and passion fruit
foam.

BRASSERIE MOLLARD

115 rue Saint-Lazare, 75008. +33 (0)1 43
87 50 22.

www.mollard.fr

This exquisite Art Nouveau treasure of
a brasserie is to be found in a rather
uninspiring setting, just across the

Helen Massy-Beresford.

road from the Gare Saint-Lazare. Step
inside to be wowed by the décor – the
flamboyant Italian mosaics, tiled scenes
and over-the-top marble and glass have
all been painstakingly restored and
it really is like stepping back in time.
Seafood is a speciality – you'll walk past
the écailler's (oyster seller) stand and
tanks of lobsters on the way in – with
a huge variety of seafood platters for
all appetites and budgets. For a sneak
peek at the lavish interior without sitting
down to a full meal, come for tea, with a
selection of pâtisseries, crêpes and ice
creams served between 3 p.m. and 7 p.m.

MINIPALAIS

Le Grand Palais, Pont Alexandre III, 3
avenue Winston Churchill, 75008. +33 (0)1
42 56 42 42

www.minipalais.com

Amid stiff competition, MINIPALAIS must
make it onto the leaderboard of Paris's
most beautiful dining spots, with its
palm-lined courtyard, grandiose marble
columns and sculpture-lined walls and
its tangles of cascading fairy lights. The
menu successfully jazzes up old-school

French cuisine with some unexpected twists: tuna tartare with ginger, coriander and spiced guacamole as a starter (€17) or a main course of roast lamb with a cumin-scented chick pea purée and padrón peppers (€35). For a quicker pit-stop after a day spent tramping the nearby Champs-Élysées or climbing the Arc de Triomphe, try Le Mini Palais for tea with a selection of homemade cakes and biscuits €14).

Best Bistrots

LES KOUPOLES
55 rue des Mathurins, 75008. +33 (0)1 42 65 31 58

Authentic Auvergne cuisine (including aligot on Tuesdays) using the finest ingredients from the region, in this old-school hang-out whose warm atmosphere belies a rather unprepossessing exterior.

À L'AFFICHE
48 rue de Moscou, 75008. +33 (0)1 45 22 02 20
www.restaurant-alaffiche.fr

This lively bistrot attracts the office crowd at lunchtime and a more relaxed clientele in the evenings, for simple food done well.

LE COLIBRI
8 place de la Madeleine, 75008. +33 (0)1 42 60 59 22

Old-fashioned bistrot serving up decent quality classic dishes, even if they are on the expensive side, in the shadow of the imposing Madeleine church. The terrace is a good spot for watching the world go by.

Helen Massy-Beresford

Al Fresco Paris

FLORA DANICA

142 avenue des Champs-Élysées, 75008.
+33 (0)1 44 13 86 26
www.floradanica.fr

For a taste of something completely different in a stunning pared back Scandinavian style, head to this Danish restaurant which has a charming and leafy multi-level terrace whose roof opens in sunny weather. The Flora Danica platter (€36) gives a taste of everything that is great about the menu here – exquisite marinated salmon, herrings and cod roe tarama. For an even more upmarket experience, the Michelin-starred Copenhague occupies the same address.

L'ORANGERIE

31 avenue George V, 75008. +33 (0)1 49 52 72 24
www.lorangerieparis.com

L'Orangerie, also within the Four Seasons, conjures up a slightly more relaxed vibe than Le Cinq.

Julien Mivielle

BLOOM PENTHIÈVRE

19 rue de Penthièvre, 75008. +33 (0)7 85
46 11 18

www.bloom-restaurant.fr

Eat healthy and eat local with the fresh
bowls, soups, sandwiches and bagels on
offer at this small chain of casual restaurants
aimed at a lunch-break crowd and also
offering a weekend brunch. There are
branches in the 6th (2 rue Guénégaud) and
the 11th (126 avenue Parmentier) as well.

LES BOLS DE JEAN

37 rue de la Boétie, 75008. +33 (0)1 42 89
28 07

www.bolsdejean.com

If you've had enough of steak frites or
onion soup this is the place for you – it's
nothing if not original. Chef Jean Imbert,
one-time winner of French reality TV
chef competition Top Chef, is the man
behind the concept and Les Bols de Jean
serves up hearty and satisfying dishes in
bread bowls. Anything from lentils with
soft-boiled egg and bacon cream to veal
stew with carrots and pickles. It's not just
any bread either, but baker Éric Kayser's
sourdough. There are also branches in
the 2nd and 9th arrondissements.

LE CAMION QUI FUME

+33 (0)1 84 16 33 75

www.lecamionquifume.com

Paris's first food truck, co-founded by

Californian chef Kristin Frederick, has
been plying the city's hungry hipsters
with succulent gourmet burgers since
2011 and has branched out into bricks-
and-mortar restaurants too (at 168
rue Montmartre in the 2nd and 66 rue
Oberkampf in the 11th).

11 place de la Madeleine, 75008 on
Tuesday and Friday lunchtimes and 132
avenue de France, 75013, every weekday
lunchtime except Monday and every
weekday evening.

See the website for details on where
else to find the truck and when.

Café Culture

HONOR

54 rue du Faubourg Saint-Honoré, 75008.
www.honor-café.com

An outdoor café space hidden away
in a courtyard – cleverly adaptable
panels allow seating to be covered or
not according to the weather. And most
importantly, great coffee as well as some
simple but tasty food – granola, cakes,
quiche and sandwiches.

BREAD & ROSES

25 rue Boissy d'Anglas, 75008. +33 (0)1 47
42 40 00
http://www.breadandroses.fr/la-carte/

Come in for the speciality breads – the
muesli bread with hazelnuts, raisins
and honey is a winner – and stay for
the carefully prepared main courses,
generous salads or club sandwiches.

Do It Yourself

MAILLE

6 place de la Madeleine, 75008. +33 (0)1
40 15 06 00
**https://fr.maille.com/blogs/boutiques/
paris-la-maison-maille-french-store**

A must for mustard fans but this
boutique offers more than that –

not only all the oils, vinegars and condiments you're ever likely to need but plenty of other gastronomic gifts too. And the interior is superb.

LA NEW CAVE

33 boulevard Malesherbes, 75008. +33 (0)1 49 24 97 02
www.lanewcave.fr

Friendly English-speaking staff will guide you through the selection process in this well-stocked wine emporium, which has a particularly good selection of champagnes from independent growers. There's often a bottle of something open for you to try or you can buy a bottle to drink on-site. They organise tasting workshops too.

FAUCHON

30 place de la Madeleine, 75008. +33 (0)1 70 39 38 00.
www.fauchon.com

This chic shop on the place de la Madeleine is a gourmet gift-giver's paradise with attractive displays of upmarket biscuits, cakes, jams, fresh deli items, wines and chocolates.

LES CAVES AUGÉ

116 boulevard Haussmann, 75008. +33 (0)1 45 22 16 97
www.cavesauges.com

This wine merchant has been supplying Parisians' cellars since 1850 and it shows – the interior is delightfully

Helen Massy-Beresford

old-fashioned and the selection and knowledge of the staff as expert as you would expect.

Perfect Pâtisseries

LADURÉE

75 avenue des Champs-Élysées, 75008. +33 (0)1 40 75 08 75

www.laduree.fr

You might find more original flavours or fluorescent colours elsewhere but the name Ladurée is still synonymous with macarons and here they're sold in an almost outlandishly ornate boutique.

Cosmopolitan Paris

TAISHO KEN

27 rue du Colisée, 75008. +33 (0)1 45 61 09 79

Old-fashioned (and cheap and cheerful for the neighbourhood) Japanese restaurant where the ramen are the main event.

THU THU 8E

33 rue de Turin, 75008.

www.thuthu8eme.fr

A simple setting for tasty Vietnamese dishes such as noodle soups, bo bun and fresh and zesty salads – great value for the area.

L'ÉTOILE MAROCAINE

56 rue Galilée, 75008. +33 (0)1 47 20 44 43

www.etoilemarocaine.com

A fine selection of Moroccan cous cous, tajines and mezze plates in an upmarket setting.

Ladurée

9th Arrondissement

WITH CHARMING FOOD shopping streets including the rue des Martyrs and the rue Cadet, not to mention the impressive food halls of the grands magasins (Paris's big department stores), there is plenty to occupy the food-focused visitor in the 9th arrondissement. It's home to one of the city's most spectacular landmarks, the Palais Garnier, the national opera house, as well as many other theatres. The northern parts of the arrondissement, just south of the boulevard de Clichy (half jokingly referred to as SoPi – South Pigalle) are a trendy little network of streets packed with upmarket boutiques, épiceries and restaurants and also the ideal place to take refuge from the touristy cobbled streets of Montmartre a little further to the north. The Grands Boulevards that charge their way through the 9th arrondissement epitomise the grandiose Haussmannian architecture the city is famous for, while the nineteenth-century covered shopping arcades, often filled with antique shops and galleries in a reminder of the district's role as the auction house area of the city are a great place to wander and stop for a bite to eat.

Pure Paris

CAFÉ DE LA PAIX
5 place de l'Opéra, 75009. +33 (0)1 40 07 36 36
www.cafedelapaix.fr

In the shadow of the ostentatiously baroque edifice of the Palais Garnier, Paris's original opera house, sits another, albeit smaller, monument to all things gilt – the Café de la Paix. As you would expect from a restaurant that proudly proclaims it was opened by the Empress Eugénie in 1862, the emphasis is on tradition – and it comes at a price. Tradition does not equal a lack of innovation, however: a starter of mushroom soup (€25) comes in the form of a cappuccino accompanied by wild mushrooms, cockles and samphire, but if you want the classics there's plenty of choice, either from the écailleur (the seafood counter) or classics à la carte, such as sole meunière (€71), which comes simply done grilled with butter and served with mashed potatoes. From the delightfully old-fashioned dessert trolley, the rhubarb and strawberry Saint-Honoré is a thing of beauty while if there's ever a time to try an Opéra cake – an intricate coffee and chocolate creation of layered almond sponge, rich ganache and glossy glaze named after the Opéra Garnier – this is it.

LE BOUILLON CHARTIER
7 rue du Faubourg Montmartre, 75009. +33 (0)1 47 70 86 29
www.bouillon-chartier.com

A real slice of an old-fashioned Paris that is becoming increasingly hard to find, Le Bouillon Chartier has been serving up simple French classics at reasonable prices since 1896. Starters, including leeks in vinaigrette, frisée salad with lardons and eggs mayonnaise, start at €1.80 and mains, including stinky andouillette sausage and choucroute, begin at €8.50. The huge mirrored dining room is now a listed monument and while the restaurant is a tourist draw it has kept its old-school Parisian charm. No reservations so be prepared to queue – service is efficient and turnover high so this is not the place for a long lunch.

Orties. Nicolas Maday

Best Bistrots

ORTIES
24 rue Rodier, 75009. +33 (0)1 45 26 86 26.
www.orties-restaurant.paris

Chef Thomas Benady has set himself the task of reducing food miles, working with producers who respect the environment and making the most of local seasonal and sometimes wild produce at Orties (the name means nettles in a nod to the plant's healing and nutritional properties, despite its reputation). The end result

is as delicious as it is worthy, with a tasting menu at €55 depending on the day's ingredients. Across the road at 15 rue Rodier, Orties Cave sells a selection of natural and biodynamic wines, fruit juices, artisanal hams, oysters, honeys and spices.

LE PANTRUCHE

3 rue Victor Massé, 75009. +33 (0)1 48 78 55 60
https://www.facebook.com/ LePantruche/

It's a mark of how seriously Paris takes its cuisine that the mayor's office publishes a list of its top 100 bistrots – Le Pantruche, a 'bistrot gourmand' in the heart of the Pigalle district, made it onto the top 100 in 2017 and it's easy to see why – original ingredients cooked with precision in a buzzing atmosphere. What more could you want? It's extremely popular so you'll need to book. The man behind Le Pantruche, Franck Baranger, is going great guns, with Le Caillebotte (8 rue Hippolyte Lebas) and La Belle Maison (4 rue de Navarin), two other masterpieces of bistronomy, also thriving in the 9th.

LA PETITE BRETONNE

53 rue des Martyrs, 75009. +33 (0)9 70 35 50 39
http://www.lapetitebretonne.eu

Delicious organic buckwheat galettes and sweet crêpes at this friendly little place with a few tables on the pavement at the front.

L'ÉLAN 9

113 rue du Faubourg Poissonnière, 75009. +33 (0)9 80 65 88 70
https://lelan9.eatbu.com/#contact

Everything is home made at this inviting bistrot, all wood floors and hanging foliage on the inside. The dishes look just as pretty – and live up to their expectations once tasted. There are small sharing plates like lemon hummus with tortilla (€8) or potato croquettes with mimolette cheese (€7) as well as an inventive full menu: think the likes of radish, walnut and beetroot ravioli (€14) for a starter or a main course of steak with sundried tomatoes, peanuts and potato foam (€26).

J'GO
4 rue Drouot, 75009. +33 (0)1 40 22 09 09
www.lejgo.com

Get a taste of the south west (that usually means plenty of duck, sausage and foie gras) at this buzzing wine bar-restaurant which prides itself on sourcing the best of the region's ingredients fairly from top quality local producers and serving it up with a touch of French flair – the south west is rugby country too.

MUSÉE DE LA VIE ROMANTIQUE
Hôtel Scheffer-Renan, 16, rue Chaptal, 75009. +33 (0)1 55 31 95 67
www.museevieromantique.paris.fr

After a browse through the collections of this charming museum, once the home of nineteenth-century painter Ary Scheffer, the salon de thé is just the place for a quick bite to eat with a tasty selection of cakes and more from the Rose Bakery team, to be enjoyed looking out over the shady and tranquil garden – positively idyllic and a rare treat in built-up Paris.

BÜL – BAR À CANNES
20 avenue Trudaine, 75009. +33 (0)1 40 16 02 74

Grab an outside table at this lovely little gluten-free and veggie café and try the sugarcane juice, the trademark energy balls or the fresh and tasty brunch offer. It's set back from the traffic on the broad and unexpectedly green avenue Trudaine, so you get a good people-watching view of the busy rue des Martyrs beyond and a few rays of sunshine if you're lucky.

HELMUT NEWCAKE
28 rue Vignon, 75009. +33 (0)9 81 31 28 31
www.helmutnewcake.com

Gluten-free pâtisseries (and some without lactose) taking in the classics like lemon meringue tart, cheesecake and éclairs as well as some more original creations: try the white chocolate and grapefruit tart. At lunchtime there's a short daily menu of entirely gluten-free dishes plus at least one dairy-free and one vegetarian option too: pad thai, Buddha bowls, quiches or polenta with vegetables.

LAÉLO

63 rue du Faubourg Poissonnière, 75009. +33 (0)1 42 29 85 29
https://www.facebook.com/ restobiolaelo

Organic, vegan and gluten-free options including sandwiches, salads and cakes as well as hot choices like vegan bourguignon, vegan ham and cheese croissants or Vietnamese bo bun at this high quality healthy fast food joint. Take-away packaging is biodegradable too.

POPOTES CANTINE RESPECTUEUSE

62 rue de Clichy, 75009. +33 (0)1 71 20 34 07.
commande.popotes.fr

Construct your lunch from the selection of bases – salad, pasta and quinoa – and additional ingredients – everything from herring to Hanoi-style beef, roasted butternut squash with honey or steamed broccoli. There are 'tartines' – open sandwiches too. Although meat, fish and dairy products feature on the menu this is a great place for vegetarians and vegans. You can order online to pick up and avoid the queue.

Pop-Up Paris

42 DEGRÉS

109 rue du Faubourg Poissonnière, 75009. +33 (0)9 73 65 77 88
www.42degres.com

The founders of 42 Degrés wanted to bring together their vegan values and their love of French gastronomy: the result is a restaurant where you can choose from the likes of chia caviar and blinis (€9) parsnip and oyster mushroom shepherd's pie (€17) or pecan nut tart with date caramel (€7), all vegan, organic, raw (the 42 in the name refers to the maximum temperature for food to be considered raw) and gluten-free. There's a €33 brunch menu at weekends.

PRIVÉ DE DESSERT

4 rue Lallier, 75009. +33 (0)1 85 15 23 73
www.privededessert.com

Chef and founder Sephora Nahon wanted to do something different – and she's certainly achieved that with the 'trompe l'œil' concept at Privé de Dessert, where the menu consists of a range of French classics crafted to look like desserts and pâtisseries. This is where Alice in Wonderland might dine if she came to Paris for the weekend and it certainly feels like you've fallen down a rabbit hole when you bite into a Saint-Honoré (normally a choux and cream confection) that turns out to be a succulent hamburger accompanied by churros-disguised fries. Salmon, wild rice, fennel and dill 'sundae' anyone? The concept has certainly got Parisians talking and

Nahon gathered together the recipes behind the restaurant in a 2014 book. Reserve if you can as it's popular.

PICTO
68 rue Lafayette, 75009
www.picto.paris

Gourmet baguettes that are ideal for a picnic. Choose from Parisian classics such as saucisson or ham and cheese, made with top-quality ingredients from carefully selected suppliers or seasonally-changing specials (a tartiflette sandwich as a winter warmer, anyone?), home made salads and desserts.

Tomato and burrata 'religieuse' and churros at Privé de Dessert Privé de dessert.

Café Culture

SOUCOUPE
33 rue du Faubourg Poissonnière, 75009.
+33 (0)1 48 00 93 64
https://www.facebook.com/Café-Soucoupe-991973480815330/

Daily changing specials, healthy soups, salads and sandwiches made from high quality often organic, often vegetarian ingredients, as well as fresh juices and cakes and cookies are on the menu in this lovely little café. Grab a table at the back for a view of the lush little courtyard garden, a rare green spot in central Paris.

KB CAFÉSHOP
53 avenue Trudaine, 75009. +33 (0)1 56 92 12 41
www.kbcafeshop.com

Casual coffee shop and café where in summer you can take a seat outside

Helen Massy-Beresford

Rose Bakery.

and enjoy the comings and goings on the rue des Martyrs, in SoPi (South Pigalle), as it's sometimes known, Paris's somewhat tongue in cheek answer to the SoHos and NoHos of New York. The district that occupies the space below the boulevard de Clichy and the more touristy Montmartre above is a food-lover's paradise of bakeries, greengrocers and cheesemongers. The quality of the coffee is the main draw at KB and you can buy it on site or through the website to roast at home.

ROSE BAKERY
46 rue des Martyrs, 75009.
www.rosebakery.fr
When British founder Rose Carrarini set up Rose Bakery on the rue des Martyrs

in 2003 her mission was to bring simple fresh, mainly organic food to a Parisian food scene that had lapsed into a certain complacency. If Parisians were sceptical about British food to start with – Rose Bakery was at the vanguard of the Parisian café revolution – they have enthusiastically embraced the creative salads, creamy risottos or crumbly-crusted quiches Rose Bakery serves up, not to mention the ever-popular scones and cakes – carrot cake is a particular hit. There are now several Rose Bakery sites including a tea room at the Bon Marché department store in the 7th (24 rue de Sèvres), a shop at 1 rue de Navarin in the 9th and a concession in the Musée de la Vie Romantique (also in the 9th at 1 rue de Chaptal).

Helen Massy-Beresford

Do It Yourself

LE PRINTEMPS DU GOÛT
64 boulevard Haussmann, 75009. +33 (0)1 42 82 50 00
www.printemps.com

The department store's brand new two-storey, 900 square metre food hall is an Aladdin's Cave of French gastronomy and more. Printemps has combed the country in search of the finest jams and honeys, pâtés, cheeses, soups, wines, sauces, biscuits, spices, mustards, bread, cakes … the list goes on. Stock up your store cupboards or choose from the wide range of fresh produce. If you feel like making a meal of it there and then the terrace has an unforgettable view over the Paris rooftops.

LA PARISIENNE
12 rue Cadet, 75009. +33 (0)1 56 92 04 75
http://www.boulangerielaparisienne. com/

Unbeatable rye, sourdough and other speciality loaves and baguettes at this award-winning bakery tucked away in the

rue Cadet, a haven of gourmet shops and tiny cafés.

LAFAYETTE GOURMET

40 boulevard Haussmann, 75009. +33 (0)1 42 82 34 56

www.galerieslafayette.com

Continue your gourmet tour of Paris's department stores with this huge space dedicated to food at the vast domed Galeries Lafayette department store. A 2,500-strong wine cellar, luxury products from the likes of Valrhona chocolates to Mariage Frères teas and a souk-style spice selection where you can buy in bulk, all make this a food destination to savour.

RAP ÉPICERIE

4 rue Fléchier, 75009. +33 (0)1 42 80 09 91

www.rapparis.fr

There's everything from panettone to pasta sauce, Chianti to cantuccini in this well-stocked Italian épicerie at the bottom of the rue des Martyrs.

Beillevaire. Helen Massy-Beresford

BEILLEVAIRE

48 rue des Martyrs, 75009. +33 (0)1 45 26 84 88

http://www.fromagerie-beillevaire.com/en

A wonderful selection from all over France and beyond awaits in this cheese shop – hardly surprising as the brand makes its own cheese, yoghurts and butter in its dairy in western France.

LA MAISON DU MIEL

24 rue Vignon, 75009. +33 (0)1 47 42 26 70

http://maisondumiel.fr

A plethora of honey and honey-based products: including a dizzying array of honeys as well as honey biscuits, honey teas, honey sweets, honey vinegars. The list goes on.

LE MARCHÉ D'ANVERS

place d'Anvers, 75009.

This thriving market takes over the place d'Anvers on Friday afternoons – the place to stock up on fruit and veg, cheese, seafood, olives and much more.

Perfect Pâtisseries

AURORE CAPUCINE
3 rue de Rochechouart, 75009. +33 (0)1 48 78 16 20
www.aurorecapucine.fr

Stepping through the blue façade is like paying a visit to an old-fashioned sweet shop, with vintage tea tins lining the walls and odd bits of bric-à-brac filling the small space. Take your pick from an array of original cakes, tarts and shortbreads made using unusual ingredients that lead to a riot of colour: fluorescent green lime tarts, cornflower-blue lavender shortbreads or delicate pink redcurrant meringue tarts.

À LA MÈRE DE FAMILLE
35 rue du Faubourg Montmartre, 75009. +33 (0)1 47 70 83 69
www.lameredefamille.com

Paris's oldest chocolatier has been operating from this site since 1761 when a young grocer set up his shop here. Over the generations as sugar became more widely available, chocolate and sweets began to dominate and today La Mère de Famille sells truffles, pralines and spreads and a whole lot more from a handful of shops across the capital and its suburbs, all in an ambience that takes you back to the shop's origins.

The facade of Paris's oldest chocolatier. Alexandre Guirkinger

MESDEMOISELLES MADELEINES
37 rue des Martyrs, 75009.
**http://www.mllesmadeleines.com/
madeleines.php**

What Marcel Proust would have made of this is anyone's guess – rather than the fragrant but humble cake that had the writer's childhood memories flooding back, the madeleines in this chic boutique on the rue des Martyrs are an altogether brasher affair, available in every flavour you can imagine: caramel, grapefruit and pamplemousse or savoury olive. There are even multi-portioned cakes made from four madeleines held together with cream, fruit puree, biscuit and chocolate. Not for the faint-hearted.

Cosmopolitan Paris

GALLIKA
7 rue Godot de Mauroy, 75009.
www.gallika.fr

Gourmet Greek street food – the Kalamaki pitta (€7), a pitta filled with grilled meat, home-made tzatziki and crunchy veg is perfect for a quick bite on the go. Try the small selection of tasty mezze or the Greek-style fries with parsley, thyme and served with tzatziki too.

PECO PECO
47 rue Jean-Baptiste-Pigalle, 75009. +33 (0)1 53 16 19 84
www.pecopeco.fr

Tuck in to Japanese street food – think ris (rice bowls) and katsu sandwiches – at this casual and tiny eatery.

PINK MAMMA
20bis rue de Douai, 75009. +33 (0)9 83 55 94 52
www.bigmammagroup.com

Part of a small and extremely popular chain of loud (décor, music, personality) and bustling Italian trattorias popping up all over Paris, Pink Mamma prides itself on the quality of its ingredients – it raises its own corn-fed cows – and the skill of its chefs who grill the enormous steaks over cherrywood and quebracho for the perfect chargrilled flavour. In a quest to bring a taste of Italian dolce vita to the grey streets of Paris the two (French) founders hit on the idea of importing not just authentic Italian ingredients (except the cows – they're raised in France) but authentic Italian staff too. Fresh pasta with truffle, mascarpone and mushrooms (€18 or €68 to serve four) is heavenly. No reservations so get in early. Also check out No Entry, the self-styled 'Italian speakeasy' in the basement.

HOLY BOL
23 passage Verdeau, 75009. +33 (0)1 47 70 08 18.
www.holybol.com

Tucked away among the antique book shops and art galleries of the Passage Verdeau shopping arcade is this bijou little restaurant which brings together Thai food and exquisite French pâtisserie, both home made.

13

10th Arrondissement

THE HIGHLIGHT OF the 10th arrondissement for most visitors is the Canal Saint-Martin, a welcome breath of air with its shady trees and green wrought-iron bridges (made famous by the scenes shot there in the film Amélie). Once a resolutely working class district of small-scale factories and workshops, the area around the canal has been gentrified beyond all recognition and its restaurants, cafés and bars draw stylish crowds on summer nights, with the party spilling over onto the banks of the canal itself, the broad sweep of cobbles at the Quai de Jemmapes as the canal turns up towards the Bassin de la Villette making the ideal spot for an impromptu picnic. There's more to the 10th than just the canal, however – the newly refurbished and partially pedestrianised place de la République has always been a focal point for Parisians, especially so since the November 2015 terror attacks that took place nearby. And while the streets around the Gare du Nord lack the charm and space of the canal, their large Indian, Bangladeshi and Sri Lankan populations make for a treasure trove of cosmopolitan eating spots. Around the Gare de l'Est is a great place to sample some of the regional specialities of the eastern parts of France such as Alsatian choucroute garnie.

Pure Paris

LE GALOPIN
34 rue Sainte-Marthe, 75010. +33 (0)1 42 06 05 03
www.le-galopin.com

This surprisingly upscale but unstuffy restaurant is tucked away a few minutes' walk from the Canal Saint-Martin in the charmingly shabby rue Sainte-Marthe. Go à la carte or choose the €58 per head tasting menu at this bistrot which really puts the gastronomy into bistronomy: think cod with Brussels sprouts, black chanterelle mushrooms and a champagne sabayon.

The flavours pop and the presentation, as you would expect from a former winner of Top Chef, is exquisite. For a more low-key taste of the same talent try La Cave à Michel, the wine bar rustling up delicious and original tapas style plates next door at number 36 where you can also choose from a fine selection of bottles.

BOUILLON JULIEN
16 rue du Faubourg Saint-Denis, 75010. +33 (0)1 47 70 12 06
www.bouillon-julien.com

It's easy to see why this place is a listed historical monument: the Art Nouveau

Bouillon Julien. Helen Massy-Beresford

décor is jaw-droppingly over-the-top. Amid the stained glass, the painted 'Flower Ladies', the mirrors and the cornicing, it's a challenge to concentrate on the food. It has recently been reinvented as a cheap and cheerful 'bouillon' – the perfect opportunity to enjoy good quality simple food in an extravagant setting.

LA STRASBOURGEOISE

5 rue du 8 mai 1945, 75010. +33 (0)1 42 05 20 02
http://strasbourgeoiseparis.com

A taste of Alsace, in the east of France just outside the Gare de l'Est station where trains to that part of the country depart and arrive. Don't miss the choucroute.

HÔTEL DU NORD

102 quai de Jemmapes, 75010. +33 (0)1 40 40 78 78.
www.hoteldurnord.org

In another cinematic link to this much-immortalised area of Paris, this elegant black-and-white-tiled Parisian space overlooking the Canal Saint-Martin was made famous by the 1938 Michel Carné film of the same name set here. The menu is a mix of some French, some not-so-French dishes: pork terrine with pickles as a starter (€9) or teriyaki tuna with spinach (€21) as a main course for example.

TERMINUS

33 rue de Dunkerque, 75010. +33 (0)1 42 85 05 15
www.terminusnord.com

Step off the train at the Gare du Nord and less than a minute later you can be immersed in the Paris of the Jazz Age, in this evocative Art Nouveau/Art Deco brasserie.

Best Bistrots

BISTRO BASQUE

20 rue du Faubourg Poissonnière, 75010. +33 (0)1 42 46 56 20

This simple venue is just the place to try out some of the regional specialities from the Basque Country, tucked down in the extreme south west of France close to the Spanish border. Try sheep's cheese served with black cherry jam, spicy sausages – Espelette pepper comes from the region – or crème catalane, a citrusy take on crème caramel. There's even a (tiny) courtyard at the back.

CHEZ MICHEL

10 rue de Belzunce, 75010. +33 (0)1 85 15 25 86.

www.restaurantchezmichel.fr

Old-world Breton specialities are on the menu at this sister restaurant to La Pointe du Grouin, with an emphasis on fish and seafood as you would expect from the little peninsular buffeted by the Atlantic. Try the Kaotriade, a Breton take on bouillabaisse or fish stew.

CHEZ CASIMIR

6 rue de Belzunce, 75010. +33 (0)1 48 78 28 80

High quality bistrot fare from another member of the rue de Belzunce Breton family – the emphasis is on good quality ever-changing ingredients cooked simply but well and served in a casual setting. At weekends there's a €30 a head buffet brunch.

CHEZ PRUNE

36 rue Beaurepaire, 75010. +33 (0)1 42 41 30 47

https://www.facebook.com/ pages/Chez-prune-Canal-St- martin/119858668096476

Come for the view – from the outside

tables in summer time you can watch the boats chug past on the Canal Saint-Martin just a few feet away – and stay for good simple food at a reasonable price for this increasingly gentrified area. There are usually cheese or charcuterie platters and a handful of daily specials plus a brunch deal. It gets crowded so come early and be prepared to wait for a table.

L'ATMOSPHÈRE

49 rue Lucien Sampaix, 75010. +33 (0)1 40 38 09 21

https://www.facebook.com/ LAtmosphère-229772823727088/

Steaks, confit duck and salads are served up in a casual setting with a vintage vibe at this low-key but popular canal-side bistrot.

Al Fresco Paris

CAFÉ A

148 rue du Faubourg Saint-Martin, 75010. +33 (0)9 81 29 83 38 for lunchtime reservations; +33 (0)7 71 61 10 38 for evening.

www.cafea.fr

Imaginative cooking (the likes of catch of the day with carrot, chickpea and wild garlic stew at €16 or duck supreme with freekeh risotto and mushroom cream at €17), organic wines and above all a stunning location in this shady courtyard of a former convent, which also hosts an arts centre and exhibitions and concerts and is sheltered from the traffic and bustle of the nearby Gare de l'Est.

PINK FLAMINGO

67 rue Bichat, 75010. +33 (0)1 42 02 31 70.
www.pinkflamingopizza.com

Good quality pizzas with flavoursome twists – the Gandhi features sag paneer, baba ganoush and paprika while for the really adventurous, the Ho Chi Minh boasts prawns and chicken in green curry sauce, coconut, peanut, lemongrass and coriander. It's a few minutes' walk away from the Canal Saint-Martin but will deliver to your chosen picnic spot by the water and there are more branches across Paris.

POINT EPHEMÈRE – LE TOP

200 quai de Valmy, 75010. +33 (0)1 40 34 02 48.
www.pointephemere.org

Get some perspective from this rooftop restaurant, part of a thriving cultural, arts and music venue on the canal.

JULES ET SHIM

22 rue des Vinaigriers, 75010.
www.julesetshim.com

Korean picnic is the concept at this bright and breezy eatery a few minutes away from the canal – and a takeaway bibimbap is perfect for an al fresco dinner by the water's edge.

Going Green

CAFÉ PINSON

58 rue du Faubourg Poissonnière, 75010.
www.cafepinson.fr

This relaxed and stylish café was set up by a food writer and blogger who wanted to demonstrate that healthy eating doesn't have to equal deprivation. Wheat-free, gluten-free, vegan, organic, superfood, raw food ... if that all sounds restrictive just give it a try – it really isn't. This is the second branch – the original, at 6 rue Forez in the 3rd arrondissement, is open in the evening too.

BOB'S JUICE BAR

15 rue Lucien Sampaix, 75010. +33 (0)9 50 06 36 18
www.bobsjuicebar.com

Homemade salmon and cream cheese bagels, smashed avocado, a wide range of veggie – and vegan-friendly dishes and great coffee from Café Lomi – not to mention the cold-pressed juices that give the spot its name, Bob's Juice Bar is a hipster's dream. Don't let that put you off: the food is good and the welcome warm. The veggie rice (€9.50), a warming gluten-free and vegan bowl of nourishing coconut milk-infused goodness topped with crushed peanut,

Helen Massy-Beresford

is a winner. If that all sounds too healthy, try a matcha chocolate cookie with your espresso.

Pop-Up Paris

APÉRO SAINT-MARTIN

104 quai de Jemmapes, 75010. +33 (0)9 81 99 98 88

http://www.aperosaintmartin.com

A light and airy concept bar based around the French apéritif: carefully selected tapenades, pâtés and wines from top producers across France line the walls – you can also buy them to take away and picnic alongside the canal – while there is a short but delicious menu of homemade small plates.

Pancake Sisters

Apéro Saint-Martin. Helen Massy-Beresford

PANCAKE SISTERS

3 rue Lucien Sampaix, 75010.
www.pancakesisters.com

You might think there's not much room for innovation in the world of pancakes, but the Pancake Sisters have managed

it, with the Panster, a pancake-sandwich hybrid offered with a daily changing variety of fillings to eat in or take away. There's also a full American-style pancake and brunch menu as well as soups, salads and granola for the more health-conscious. There's also a branch in the 11th at 11 rue Popincourt.

BOL

76 rue du Faubourg Poissonnière, 75010.
+33 (0)1 42 46 39 27
www.bolporridgebar.com

This porridge bar offers an alternative
to the more usual Parisian breakfast
of tartines and croissants (or espresso
and a cigarette) – healthy fresh hot
porridge bowls with original ingredients
such as pear and lychee compote and
spirulina or homemade nutella as well
as overnight oats, granola and savoury
bowls too.

LA POINTE DU GROUIN

8 rue de Belzunce, 75010. 01 48 78 28 80
https://www.lapointedugrouin.com

A one-of-a-kind concept sees your
usual euros converted into 'grouins' in
a special machine at this modern take
on a Breton tavern. One grouin equals
one euro and once the transaction is
completed, you can exchange them for
cider (of course), Breton beer or wine
as well as a Breton take on tapas-style

La Pointe du Grouin. Julien Mivielle

small plates – try the Galette saucisse
Breizh (Breton sausage pancake)
at €6. This is a welcome addition
to the sometimes rather lacklustre
restaurants crowding around the
Gare du Nord and just the place to
while away your last minutes in Paris
before taking the Eurostar. It's also an
ideal spot to try a Kouign Amman, the
deliciously buttery Breton speciality
pastry (€2). This is a third Breton
venture in the same street from the
appropriately named Thierry Breton.

Café Culture

HOLYBELLY

5 rue Lucien Sampaix, 75010.
https://holybellycafe.com

Part of a wave of casual, international hangouts serving top-quality food and coffee that has swept through Paris in recent years, Holybelly is inspired by a Melbourne-style café and is the place to go for pancake-stack breakfasts, great coffee as well as classic French dishes with a twist. They don't take reservations and there's almost always a queue, but with good reason.

Fabien-Courmont

CHEZ JEANNETTE

47 rue du Faubourg Saint-Denis, 75010.
+33 (0)1 47 70 30 89

Vintage décor and a young crowd combine at this neighbourhood café/bar, where there's a good choice of tapas to go with your apéritif.

LA SARDINE

32 rue Sainte-Marthe, 75010. +33 1 42 49 19 46
http://barlasardine.com/restaurant-place-sainte-marthe/

Friendly and fun neighbourhood bar with simple tapas-style food on the charming little place Sainte-Marthe.

Do It Yourself

MARCHÉ SAINT-QUENTIN

85bis boulevard de Magenta, 75010. +33 (0)1 48 85 93 30

Stock up on fresh fruit and veg, cheese, charcuterie and wine at this authentic Parisian market where locals come to buy the ingredients for their Sunday lunch (it closes at 13.30 on Sundays). Or visit one of the casual food stands – everything from Brazilian to Moroccan, Lebanese to Portuguese – eat on the spot or take away. Just a short walk from the Gare du Nord, this is an ideal place to stock up on last-minute Parisian treats before taking the Eurostar.

LE VERRE VOLÉ

67 rue de Lancry, 75010. +33 (0)1 48 03 17 34
www.leverrevole.fr

If you've thought ahead and brought a corkscrew (screw tops are still pretty rare in France) you can pick up a bottle of something wonderful – there's a wide choice with many organic and natural wines – and enjoy it sitting by the nearby Canal Saint-Martin. This lovely little wine shop also offers simple dishes and sharing platters to accompany wines by the glass if it's not picnic weather. Don't be fooled by the casual vibe, Le Verre Volé can get busy so it's wise to book if you want to eat here.

Perfect Pâtisseries

DU PAIN ET DES IDÉES

34 rue Yves Toudic, 75010. +33 (0)1 42 40 44 52

www.dupainetdesidees.com

One of Paris's best bakeries, both for the quality of the bread and for the charmingly old-fashioned shopfront and interior. Check out the traditional Galette des Rois – a frangipane puff pastry tart sold with a paper crown and a little charm baked inside to celebrate Epiphany. These are available at bakeries all over France for the whole month of January but this one is exceptional.

Cosmopolitan Paris

MAMAGOTO

5 rue des Petits Hôtels, 75010. +33 (0)1 44 79 03 98

http://www.mamagoto.fr

A relaxed setting for delicate and tasty Franco-Japanese fusion.

RAVIOLI CHINOIS NORD-EST

11 rue Civiale, 75010. +33 (0)1 75 50 88 03

If the décor and the service are nothing to write home about, the tasty and fragrant dim-sum style dumplings plus a few soups and side salads are worth the cramped tables and inevitable queue (no bookings). It's cheap too, with a plate of ten dumplings at €5. Try pork, white cabbage and mushroom or beef and turnip.

Julien Mivielle

KRISHNA BHAVAN

24 rue Cail, 75010, +33 (0)1 42 05 78 43

www.krishna-bhavan.com

This Indian restaurant is one, or more accurately, several of the highlights of the 'Little India' in the streets around the Gare du Nord – there are three branches on the same street plus an outlier on the Left Bank, in the 5th arrondissement (25 rue Galande). The thali at €14 is a great deal including poppadum, raita, rice, chapathi and a selection of curries. Try the dosas, rice and lentil flour based pancakes ideal for dipping in the aromatic sauces. An extensive and entirely vegetarian menu makes this a great option for visiting veggies.

LE PETIT CAMBODGE

20 rue Alibert, 75010. +33 (0)1 42 45 80 88.
https://lepetitcambodge.fr

'Little Cambodia''s bright yellow awning shines like a ray of sunshine against the grey backdrop of Paris, and the food will brighten up your day too. But its sunny exterior belies a sad recent history. Le Petit Cambodge was one of the unlucky targets of the 13 November 2015 terrorist attacks in Paris when gunmen attacked the crowds of young Parisians out dining and drinking in this lively district. Like the other restaurants and bars in the surrounding streets and in the neighbouring 11th arrondissement that were affected, the team at Le Petit Cambodge were adamant the terrorists would not stop them. The restaurant kept its vibrant yellow awning but revamped its interior and reopened a few months later to delight from locals missing their bo bun fix. It's as popular as ever but if you leave your number the staff will call you when a table is free. There's another branch on the nearby rue Beaurepaire too as well as Le Cambodge, the slightly more formal member of the family a stone's throw away on avenue Richerand.

LA MADONNINA

10 rue Marie et Louise, 75010. +33 (0)1

The short menu at this neighbourhood Italian restaurant features stuzzichini or Italian tapas style dishes such as grilled

Helen Massy-Beresford

scamorza with rocket and burratina with truffle; well-thought-out pasta dishes such as rigatoni with asparagus and pancetta (€15) as well as carpaccios and salads. The quality of the ingredients, the presentation and the sleek Parisian setting elevate a trip to a traditional Italian trattoria into something a bit special.

THE SUNKEN CHIP
39 rue des Vinaigriers, 75010. +33 1 53 26 74 46.
www.thesunkenchip.com

Parisians greeted the arrival of the city's first fish-and-chip shop The Sunken Chip, in 2013, with glee, flocking to try traditional fish-and-chips, complete with mushy peas – although it must be said, purée de petits pois does sound much more sophisticated. There are classics like hake in beer batter (€12.50 with chips) and more unusual offerings – coley in cornflake and parsley batter (€12 with chips). Eat at one of the long sharing benches in the restaurant or take your fish-and-chips to the banks of the canal, enjoying the contrast between British taste and French atmosphere. Such has been its success that The Sunken Chip van now tours France bringing vinegar-soaked delights to events and festivals across the country.

LE BISTROT MME SHAWN
3 rue des Récollets, 75010. +33 (0)1 46 07 02 00
www.mmeshawn.com

Step inside this welcoming industrial-meets-vintage space, with its wooden floors, mismatched furniture and bric-à-brac décor for relaxed and friendly service and good quality Thai food. Main courses are around €15. This is just one of a small chain of Thai restaurants and bistrots in first, third, eleventh and seventeenth arrondissements as well as in Bangkok, and this branch is in a perfect spot – its big windows look out towards the curve of the Canal Saint-Martin.

Bistrot Mme Shawn. Helen Massy-Beresford

14

11th Arrondissement

DENSELY POPULATED AND full of bars, restaurants and clubs, the 11th is one of the liveliest areas of Paris, with nightlife concentrated in several sub-districts, around the rue Oberkampf, the place de la Bastille, the rue du Faubourg Saint-Antoine and the boulevard Voltaire where there are myriad restaurants catering to every taste and budget. As a formerly scruffy – and cheap – area that has rapidly gentrified, the 11th has been the crucible of many of Paris's restaurant trends in the past 10-15 years, with the craze for bistronomy style cooking, gourmet burgers, small sharing plates and vegan cuisine all making their mark here. That culinary innovation is now increasingly taking place in other cheaper districts but the 11th is still a melting pot of dining options for all tastes, styles and budgets.

Pure Paris

LE CHATEAUBRIAND

129 avenue Parmentier, 75011. +33 (0)1 43 57 45 95

https://lechateaubriand.net

The name and the setting – and the sheer quality of the gastronomy on offer may be very French – but perhaps it's because chef Iñaki Aizpitarte comes from the Basque Country, with its strong regional identity, that there are so many and varied influences both in the outstanding and innovative cuisine – a fixed menu at €75 – and the wine list, which is dominated by organic and biodynamic varieties from all across the globe.

SEPTIME

80 rue de Charonne, 75011. +33 (0)1 43 67 38 29
www.septime-charonne.fr

Head to the in-demand, one Michelin-starred Septime if you can – you may

Duck with roasted shallots, fig and juniper. Septime

Septime. F. Flohic

need to work some magic to get a table – for the extraordinary gastronomic tasting menu at €80 a head (an extra €55 if you want wine pairings too). La Cave du Septime (just around the corner at 3 rue Basfroi) is the ideal place to while away the time waiting for a table to be free.

La Cave du Septime. Septime

Best Bistrots

LE BEAU MARCHÉ
90 boulevard Beaumarchais, 75011. +33 (0)9 83 60 41 26
https://www.facebook.com/pg/ RestoLeBeauMarche/reviews/

It's a classic formula – but it works: simple dishes that put top quality ingredients in the spotlight, French classics with little modern twists. And all served with a smile. Think tender beef slowly braised in Brouilly wine served with garlicky white mogette beans (€23) or scallops served with a turnip mousse and grilled hazelnuts (€25). The atmosphere is relaxed and the comfortable enclosed terrace out front is an ideal place to while away a few hours.

MONSIEUR EDGAR
35 rue Faidherbe, 75011. +33 (0)1
http://www.monsieuredgarbistrot.fr
There's something for everyone here:
tapas, salads a meat-heavy main dish
selection and home-made desserts.

LE BISTROT DU PEINTRE
116 avenue Ledru-Rollin, 75011. +33 (0)1
47 00 34 39
www.bistrotdupeintre.com
Good quality ingredients, simply but
beautifully cooked in this old-fashioned
and welcoming neighbourhood bistrot.
Menus change daily with starters around
€6 and main courses at about €14.

CLAMATO
80 rue de Charonne, 75011. +33 (0)1
http://www.clamato-charonne.fr
The Clamato-Septime-La Cave trinity is
a byword for gastronomic excellence in

Ceviche at Clamato. B. Schmuck

*Merlan colbert with tartare sauce – Clamato's
answer to fish and chips.* S. Monjanel

this little corner of Paris, and beyond. At
Clamato, you'll be served small plates
of exquisitely flavourful and beautifully
presented seafood – rillettes, carpaccio,
ceviche – with a fine wine selection (with
many natural wines) to match.

LE PURE CAFÉ
14 rue Jean Macé, 75011. +33 (0)1 43 71 47 22
http://www.lepurecafe.fr
Hawaiian poke bowls sit side-by-
side with côtes de bœuf on the mix-
and-match menu at this lovely little
neighbourhood bistrot. The décor is
100 per cent traditional Paris, however,
and the terrace is perfect for people-
watching.

Al Fresco Paris

LE PERCHOIR
14 rue Crespin du Gast, 75011. +33 (0)1 48 06 18 48
www.leperchoir.tv

A truly panoramic view across the city at this rooftop bar and restaurant run by the team behind Le Pavillon Puebla in the Parc des Buttes-Chaumont.

AL TAGLIO
2bis rue Neuve-Popincourt, 75011. +33 (0)1 43 38 12 00
https://www.facebook.com/AlTaglio.fr/

Pizza by the slice, Italian style, with a few terrace tables out front.

GREENHOUSE
22 rue Crespin du Gast, 75011. +33 (0)9 80 48 79 47
www.greenhousecafe.fr

GreenHouse is the latest offering from Californian chef Kristin Frederick, the woman behind gourmet burger food truck Le Camion Qui Fume. Here it's all about top quality ingredients and round-the-world influences: everything from Japanese-style gyozas to South American-influenced corncakes. The team makes use of its urban vegetable garden – you can grab a table outside near to it to soak up the sun and the urban green vibe – to ensure it provides diners with organic, balanced and healthy delights.

Going Green

BEARS AND RACCOONS
21 rue Richard Lenoir, 75011. +33 (0)9 51 67 87 71
www.bearsandraccoons.com

Healthy fast-food – or 'fast-good' – in the heart of the 11th with a range of generously-filled sandwiches and cakes as well as a grocery corner where you can stock up on gluten-free goodies.

CHAMBELLAND
14 rue Ternaux, 75011. +33 (0)1 43 55 07 30
www.chambelland.com

This naturally gluten-free and organic bakery has got Parisians, addicted to their baguettes and croissants, talking.

SOYA
20 rue de la Pierre Levée, 75011. +33 (0)1 48 06 33 02
www.soya-cantine-bio.fr

The décor may be pared back in this loft-style space but the flavours are all here:

SOYA

Masala curry at SOYA. SOYA

sandwiches that go a step beyond the jambon-beurre or poulet-crudités you'll find in nearly every bakery. Try the baguette with smoky morteau sausage, gribiche sauce and pickles (€7). Or pick your own ingredients from the likes of Fourme d'Ambert or St Nectaire cheese, Prince de Paris ham or chorizo (€5.50 for two ingredients). There are salads and other small bites including a daily special such as rabbit with mushrooms (€10) and classic desserts like vanilla rice pudding (€5).

JONES
43 rue G. Cavaignac, 75011. +33 (0)9 80 75 32 08
www.jonescaferestaurant.com

Small sharing plates with fresh, seasonal and often unusual ingredients are the order of the day in this casual spot in the 11th. Don't let having to Google the likes of 'bastelle blette et brocciu' (a type of Corsican pastry filled with cheese and vegetables) before you order put you off. Staff are only too happy to explain the more obscure dishes, suggest a matching wine from the good wine list and don't mind if you order a few dishes at a time to match your dinner to your appetite.

LE FOOD MARKET
boulevard de Belleville, 75011, between Couronnes and Ménilmontant metro stations.
http://www.lefoodmarket.fr

A lively street food market made up of stalls offering everything from Vietnamese nems to Mexican burritos

big crunchy salads, curries, vegetable gratins and plenty of small plates to share inspired by veggie-friendly cuisines the world over. Nearly everything is gluten-free too.

Pop-Up Paris

CHEZALINE
85 rue de la Roquette, 75011. +33 (0)1 43 71 90 75
In the unusual setting of a former horsemeat butcher's shop, you'll find

with big sharing tables to sit down and enjoy your selection. It's usually every Thursday evening but check out the website for more details.

FULGURANCES

10 rue Alexandre Dumas, 75011. +33 (0)1 43 48 14 59

http://fulgurances.com/en/

With a new resident chef every few months, it's impossible to know what to expect from Fulgurances – which styles itself as a 'chef incubator' giving young kitchen talents a chance to hone their craft – except that it will be delicious.

Café Culture

TEN BELLES BREAD

17-19bis rue Breguet, 75011. +33 (0)9 67 86 08 19

If Parisians, scarred by language exchanges before the food revolution took hold in Britain, are occasionally sceptical about British cuisine, this does not apply to baking and desserts. This inviting bakery and coffee shop is run by one Franco-British and one British chef, who have been making their mark on the Paris gastronomy scene and the influences from across the channel are obvious here: scones, Eton mess and savoury pies are all delicious and the range of breads from simple sourdough to the likes of sprouted rye bread give Parisian institutions a run for their money. The coffee from Café Lomi is excellent. There's another branch, this one more a coffee shop but still with

a great selection of pastries and tarts, just a stone's throw from the Canal Saint-Martin in the 10th at 10 rue de la Grange aux Belles.

CAFÉ CHARBON

109 rue Oberkampf, 75011. +33 (0)1 43 57 55 13

www.lecafecharbon.fr

This lovely café, which dates from 1863, has moved with the times – it's now something of a hub for this lively drinking, dancing and dining district.

Do It Yourself

MARCHÉ PÈRE LACHAISE

boulevard de Ménilmontant, between rue des Panoyaux and rue des Cendriers, 75011. +33 (0)1 43 24 74 39

An authentic market on the boulevard frequented by locals stocking up on fresh and regional produce.

Artisan fruit juices on a market stall. Helen Massy-Beresford

ÉPICERIE ET ASSOCIÉS

25 rue Faidherbe, 75011. +33 (0)1 43 71 02 41
http://www.epicerieetassocies.com

If this tiny space is home to some of
the finest cheeses, cured meats, pickles,
conserves, wines and more that you
could hope to find, that's because the
team has dedicated itself to searching
out the best small independent
producers from every corner of France.
An ideal place to pick up a takeaway
sandwich, salad or deli selection for a
picnic. There's another branch in the 8th
at 8 rue de Castellane.

LE VIN QUI PARLE

30 rue Faidherbe, 75011. +33 (0)1 43 56 38 53
www.levinquiparle.fr

Themed wine tastings take place every
other Saturday afternoon at this well-
stocked wine shop that prides itself on
the good value choices filling its shelves.

Cosmopolitan Paris

BLUE ELEPHANT

43-45 rue de la Roquette, 75011. +33 (0)1
47 00 42 00
www.blueelephant.com

An extensive and flavourful Thai menu
awaits you in this exuberantly decorated
space, all bamboo and carved wood.
Try the lamb massaman (€23.50) a rich
and spicy speciality from the south of
Thailand or the Coco Cabane (€27) a green
curry from Phuket served in a coconut
shell or go for one of the selection
platters if the choice is too much.

LA BAGUE DE KENZA

106 rue Saint-Maur, 75011. +33 (0)1 43 14 93 15
www.labaguedekenza.com

More than 200 types of sweet and savoury
Algerian pastries – available to take away or
enjoy in the tea salon with a pot of mint tea.

L'ÉQUATEUR

151 rue Saint-Maur, 75011. +33 (0)1 43 57 99 22
www.lequateur.fr

This wonderful pan-African spot serves
up favourites from Cameroon, Senegal
and Ivory Coast as well as local beers
and South African wines.

ACQUA E FARINA

38 rue Faidherbe, 75011. +33 (0)1 44 62 69 40
www.acquaefarinaparis.com

Excellent pizza (made by a Neopolitan
pizzaiolo) as well as pasta and salads in
this modern space where the quality of
the ingredients is the top priority.

CAFÉ TITON

34 rue Titon, 75011. +33 (0)9 53 17 94 10
http://cafetiton.com

A cosy and relaxed German café where you
can get your fix of curry wurst, apple strudel
and a choice of over thirty German beers.

Emilie-Albert-SD

12th Arrondissement

THE 12TH ARRONDISSEMENT, lacking the big must-see sights that draw tourists to more central districts, rarely makes it on to tourists' itineraries. This is a shame. It might not boast an Eiffel Tower or a Louvre, but the great green expanse of the Bois de Vincennes which begins in the east of the arrondissement and stretches out beyond the city limits gives an entirely different perspective on an intensely urban capital city. As does the Promenade Plantée, also known as the Coulée Verte René Dumont, a disused railway converted into an inviting flower-lined walkway that starts near Bastille in the 11th arrondissement and winds its way above the streets of the 12th. Both are wonderful spots for a picnic. Foodwise, the highlight is the marché d'Aligre, where you can find everything you need to get your tastebuds going, but there are plenty of neighbourhood restaurants and bars that are worth a detour too.

Pure Paris

LE TRAIN BLEU
Gare de Lyon, place Louis Armand, 75012. +33 (0)1 43 43 09 06.
www.le-train-bleu.com

For fans of the classic Parisian brasserie, Le Train Bleu is simply unmissable. Cross the threshold from the busy Gare de Lyon into another time. This brasserie behemoth was opened in 1901 after the station had been renovated for the 1900 Universal Exhibition. It was renamed in 1963, the blue a nod to the trains departing for the Côte d'Azur. Inside, the gilt, chandeliers and mirrors border on the overwhelming but the menu is

enticing, with brasserie favourites bien sûr but also signs of moving with the times: celeriac, leek tofu and artichoke lasagne with a truffle sauce as a vegetarian option (€29) being one of them.

Best Bistrots

LE SQUARE TROUSSEAU
1 rue Antoine Vollon, 75012. +33 (0)1 43 43 06 00.
www.squaretrousseau.com

Delicious inventive versions of French classics, unobtrusive but helpful service, first-rate ingredients, an attractive wine list and all in a quiet setting looking out over the Square

Le Square Trousseau. Helen Massy-Beresford

Armand Trousseau. Just lovely.

TABLE
3 rue de Prague, 75012. +33 (0)1 4343 1226
www.tablerestaurant.fr

As you would hope, sitting down to eat just minutes from the market (le marché d'Aligre) translates into simple dishes that leave room for the fresh and fine ingredients to make their mark. With starters around the €20 mark and main courses anything from €39 upwards this is a place to savour, but well worth the price tag – and the old-style zinc bar and brasserie décor add to the special occasion feel.

AMARANTE
4 rue Biscornet, 75012. +33 (0)7
www.amarante.paris

Tucked away in a back street a short walk from the bustle of the place de la Bastille you'll find hearty dishes such as Challandais duck roasted with beetroot or Dordogne guinea fowl with spelt and a great selection of wines by the glass. With main courses à la carte at €25, the €22 lunchtime menu looks particularly good value. The chocolate mousse (€10) made using cocoa from São-Tomé-and-Principe has acquired something of a reputation in the Paris food scene.

Al Fresco Paris

LE CHALET DES ÎLES DAUMESNIL
Ile de Reuilly, Bois de Vincennes, 75012.
+33 (0)1 43 07 00 10
http://www.lechaletdesiles.com

A menu of brasserie classics is all very well but you'll come here for the setting, not the food. It's rare to be able to listen to birdsong and the wind swishing through the trees in Paris, but on this little island in the lake that's exactly what you can expect.

SCOTTA
11bis rue de Cotte, 75012. +33 (0)1 46 28 01 65
https://www.restaurantscotta.com

Urban vegetation a few minutes' walk from the marché d'Aligre at this lovely little Italian place with a peaceful and jungly terrace at the back. The pizza is great too and there's a good selection of Italian and French wines.

Going Green

GENTLE GOURMET

24 boulevard de la Bastille, 75012. +33 (0)1 43 43 48 49.

https://gentlegourmet.fr/

Gentle Gourmet has been showing Parisians it's possible to eat well – and gastronomically – without animal products since 2009.

Helen Massy-Beresford

COMPTOIR VEGGIE

75 avenue Ledru-Rollin, 75012. +33 (0)1 71 26 56 82

https://www.facebook.com/ comptoirveggie/

Vegan buddha bowls and juices, cakes and porridge, a weekend brunch and top-quality coffee that, if ordered to take away, comes in a fully compostable cup. Perfect.

Do It Yourself

MARCHÉ BEAUVAU (MARCHÉ D'ALIGRE)

Place d'Aligre, 75012.

A true Aladdin's Cave of gourmet gems – this huge market, spread across the indoor galleries and the adjacent sprawling outdoor space, has everything you could think of: exotic herbs and spices, olives, cheeses, coffee, wines from all over the world ... the list goes on. The flea market stalls and shops are

the perfect place to add a French touch to your table setting.

CURRY STREET

30 rue Traversière, 75012. +33 (0)9 52 41 65 99

https://www.currystreet.fr

This Indian grocery story offers simple dishes to eat in and a wealth of spices and other cooking supplies to buy.

GOURMET GOURMAND

12 rue Parrot, 75012. +33 (0)1 46 28 13 50
https://www.gourmet-gourmand.fr

This well stocked wine shop and deli offers Friday night wine tastings and light meals onsite at lunch time as well as a great selection of deli products – ham, pâtés, Italian antipasto-style grilled peppers, artichokes and olives...

Perfect Pâtisseries

AUX MERVEILLEUX DE FRED

12 place d'Aligre, 75012. +33 (0)1 43 43 67 64
www.auxmerveilleux.com

One of a handful of Parisian outposts of Frédéric Vaucamp's meringue-based empire, this little boutique specialises in the northern French and Belgian speciality of merveilleux (which literally translates as marvellous – if you have

Les Merveilleux de Fred. Helen Massy-Beresford

a sweet tooth they certainly are) – little puffs of meringue, whipped cream, crunchy biscuit and chocolate in various flavours. There's a selection of brioche-style 'cramiques' too – chocolate, sugar or raisin.

Cosmopolitan Paris

BAR À MOMOS

218 rue du Faubourg Saint-Antoine, 75012. Tibetan ravioli (momos) are the main draw, unsurprisingly at this simple little eatery. The €11 menu with soup, momos and salad is a great deal and this is a fabulous option for vegetarians.

LE TOUAREG

228 rue de Charenton, 75012. +33 (0)1 43 07 68 49
http://restaurant-letouareg.fr/fr

Good quality North African cuisine in a welcoming atmosphere.

16

13th Arrondissement

THE 13TH ARRONDISSEMENT has plenty to tempt the food-loving visitor away from the busier and more central Parisian arrondissements. Sprawling across the south eastern part of the city and with a long stretch of the Seine as its northern border, the 13th is a mix of old and new with the sleek modern architecture (supposedly designed to look like books) of the François-Mitterand national library contrasting with the quaint cobbles of the Butte aux Cailles. This latter district is a great hunting ground for gourmet discoveries while the 13th's other major foodie attraction is an Asian district, home to myriad Vietnamese, Lao, Chinese and Thai restaurants, grocery stores and take-aways. The 'Choisy triangle' as it is known is the largest of the city's 'Chinatowns' and some would argue the best place to sample some of the eastern cuisines France has embraced enthusiastically since the beginning of significant waves of immigration from France's former colonies began in the 1970s. For a trip back to a Paris from years past head to the Butte aux Cailles, a charming little hill full of cobbled streets that has kept its village feel despite gentrifying rapidly in recent years.

Pure Paris

AU PETIT MARGUÉRY RIVE GAUCHE
9 boulevard de Port-Royal, 75013. +33 (0)1 43 31 58 59
http://petitmarguery-rivegauche.com
A little enclave of starched white table linen and hyper-traditional French cuisine: rabbit terrine with hazelnuts, calf's head, Grand Marnier soufflé. The €41.50 a head menu includes three courses plus a bottle of wine to share between two and coffee and petits fours.

Best Bistrots

CHEZ GLADINES
30 rue des Cinq Diamants, 75013.
http://chezgladines-butteauxcailles.fr/en
Try specialities from the Basque Country at this casual eatery with a great selection of foie gras and other charcuterie and traditional dishes such as piperade, a tasty mixture of tomatoes, onions and peppers here served with eggs. Try some sheep's cheese with cherry jam or a cherry-filled gâteau basque to finish off your journey to the south-west.

DES CRÊPES ET DES CAILLES

13 rue de la Butte aux Cailles, 75013. +33 (0)1 45 81 68 69

Tiny and friendly little crêperie with a short selection of savoury and sweet pancakes and ciders to go with them.

SIMONE

33 boulevard Arago, 75013. +33 (0)1 43 37 82 70

http://www.simoneparis.com

Friendly neighbourhood bistrot in a quiet part of the 13th, with tables on the pavement. Four courses at €49 a head will see a riot of flavours, all homemade and using the best seasonal ingredients, presented with flair. There's also a Simone wine shop nearby at 48 rue Pascal, also in the 13th.

Simone

LES TEMPS DES CERISES

18-20 rue de la Butte aux Cailles, 75013. +33 (0)1 45 89 69 48

https://www.letempsdescerisescoop.com

The space, the décor, the menu (think roast pork and clafoutis for dessert), everything screams Paris past in this cooperative bistrot which started life as a quick canteen-style place for local factory employees to have lunch and has kept its working class values despite the area's gentrification.

Going Green

L'INCUBATEUR DE FRAÎCHEUR

151 rue du Chevaleret, 75013. 06 64 81 27 08

https://www.facebook.com/ incubateurdefraicheur/

A short but sweet menu of eclectic veggie and vegan dishes served in a casual space – think soups, salads, wraps, dal, toasties or pasta. Stock up on ingredients to cook yourself in the grocery section.

SEASON SQUARE

13 rue Louise Weiss, 75013. +33 (0)9 86 72 86 15

https://www.facebook.com/ seasonsquarerestaurant/

Hearty vegan and veggie burgers served in home made brioche plus a wide selection of fresh and healthy bowls, sweet treats and some gluten-free options to boot.

Pop-Up Paris

TOOQ TOOQ

MK2 Bibliothèque, 128 avenue de France, 75013
http://www.t88q.fr

The space outside the national library is something of a street-food hub, with a selection of food trucks selling a wide variety of cuisines. Tooq Tooq specializes in fresh and zingy authentic pad Thai and more, from noodles to salads. Check out the website for details on where to find the van – its location may change.

NEW SOUL FOOD

MK2 Bibliothèque, 128 avenue de France, 75013.
http://newsoulfood.fr

African fusion is the concept at this tempting food truck: you can smell the charcoal grilling as you approach and none of the choices – Afro-Caribbean, Afro-Subsaharan and Afro-European – disappoints. Check out the website for details of where to find it and when.

LA BRIGADE

MK2 Bibliothèque, 128 avenue de France, 75013.
www.la-brigade.fr

Definitely one for carnivores only – La Brigade serves up sliced grilled top-quality meat (choose from duck breast, onglet steak, breaded chicken...), homemade sauce, chips and salad in a takeaway carton with handy chopsticks. Check out the website to be sure the food truck is there on your chosen day. There's also a permanent branch at 103 rue Oberkampf in the 11th.

LA FELICITÀ

5 parvis Alan Turing, 75013.
www.lafelicita.fr

The latest opening from the team behind the Big Mamma group of restaurants is a cavernous space located on the Station F start-up campus with an exuberant vibe – two refurbished railway carriages form part of the décor. Foodwise,

Big Mamma

Ceviche. Big Mamma

there's something for everyone, with the space laid out in a food market style and separate stands for high-quality burgers, focaccias, pizza, bars and even a barbecue on the terrace.

Café Culture

L'AROBASE CAFÉ
101 rue du Chevaleret, 75013. +33 (0)1 45 86 64 09
http://www.arobasecafe.com
Casual and friendly neighbourhood café with outside tables and a good weekend brunch.

LE MERLE MOQUEUR
11 rue de la Butte aux Cailles, 75013.
Friendly and casual neighbourhood bar and café.

Do It Yourself

TANG FRÈRES
168 avenue de Choisy, 75013. +33 (0)1 44 24 06 72.
http://www.tang-freres.fr
Fans of Asian food flock from all over Paris and beyond to stock up at this vast Asian supermarket.

LES ABEILLES
21 rue de la Butte aux Cailles, 75013. +33 (0)1 45 81 43 48
www.lesabeilles.biz
A honey-lover's paradise, Les Abeilles was set up with the aim of bringing all the benefits of honey and honey-based products to the general public – if it's honey-related, it's here. The shop even sells beekeeping equipment as well as acacia and chestnut honey on tap and of course a vast selection of honeys, honey sweets, honey cakes, honey vinegars and more...

Perfect Pâtisseries

GÉRARD MULOT
93 rue de la Glacière, 75013. +33 (0)1 45 81 39 09
http://maison-mulot.com
Around twenty different flavours of exemplary macarons vie for your attention in this top-quality pâtisserie: try strawberry-champagne or grapefruit-pear. That's not all – there's a wonderful selection of bread, tarts and cakes including Alsace speciality the sticky raisin-studded kouglof. There's another

branch in the 6th at 76 rue de Seine and a tea salon at 12 rue des Quatre Vents.

LAURENT DUCHÊNE

2 rue Wurtz, 75013. +33 (0)1 45 65 00 77
https://www.laurentduchene.com

Quirky designs and top quality ingredients combined with skill by this prize-winning pâtissier are a winning combination.

Cosmopolitan Paris

PHO BANH CUON 14

129 avenue de Choisy, 75013. +33 (0)1 45 83 61 15

A temple to the wholesome spicy warming pho soup that in Vietnam is eaten for breakfast – enjoy it here for lunch or dinner, with banh cuon steamed pancakes, the other house speciality.

DÉLICES DE SHANDONG

88 boulevard de l'Hôpital, 75013. +33 (0)1 45 87 23 37
http://www.deliceshandong.com

Authentic offal-heavy cuisine from the Shandong province of China.

XINH XINH

8 rue des Wallons, 75013. +33 (0)1 42 18 16 92
http://restaurantxinhxinh.fr/en/gallery

You'll find all the Vietnamese classics – banh cuon, bo bun and pho and more – on the menu at this delicious little spot in the 13th.

TRICOTIN

15 avenue de Choisy, 75013. +33 (0)1 45 84 74 44
https://www.facebook.com/ TricotinParis13/

This Cantonese restaurant, which also serves some specialities from elsewhere in the region – try the Cambodian noodle soup – is the place to come for huge spicy bowls of nourishing broth and slippery noodles.

17

14th Arrondissement

THE BUZZING MARKET street rue Daguerre is a lively heart in one of the capital's quieter arrondissements, quiet being a particularly apt description given that two of its main tourist attractions are the Cimetière de Montparnasse – resting place of Simone de Beauvoir, Jean Paul Sartre and Charles Baudelaire – and the Paris Catacombs – the sprawling underground network of tunnels that has been home to millions of skeletons since city authorities began clearing the overflowing graveyards in the eighteenth century. The food shops and restaurants set out on the following pages should bring you back to life after a morning of more sombre visits and choosing the ingredients for a picnic in the market street of rue Daguerre to be enjoyed in the charming parc Montsouris will give you another perspective on this corner of the city.

Pure Paris

LA COUPOLE
102 boulevard du Montparnasse, 75014.
+33 (0)1
www.lacoupole-paris.com

If the walls of La Coupole could talk they'd have quite some stories to tell. Set up by two brothers from the Auvergne – a region that has given Paris many of its restaurateurs, as sons and daughters left ailing farming communities to build new lives – the mosaics, marble pillars and Art Déco style of this buzzing brasserie have welcomed everyone from Josephine Baker to Picasso, Henry Miller to Matisse, Serge Gainsbourg, Jane Birkin, Albert Camus … the list goes on. Life is a bit more sedate at La Coupole these days, though not for the waiters,

Yann Deret

La Coupole, Paris. Yann Deret

still spinning around between starched white tables, wielding huge trays full of ice-packed platters of mussels, steaming choucroutes and frothy beers.

LE ZEYER

62 rue d'Alésia, 75014. +33 (0)1 45 40 43 88
www.lezeyer.com

This brasserie is Parisian to its very core – choose from classics such as steak tartare or choucroute or pick one of the daily-changing fish dishes that depend on the catch of the day.

Best Bistrots

LES FAUVES

33 boulevard Edgar Quinet, 75014. +33 (0)1 72 38 58 92
www.lesfauves.paris

Big colourful salads, sharing plates with a difference (charcuterie and cheese versions but also tuna tataki with chia, spring onions, ginger and beansprouts) plus a full menu of constantly changing starters, mains and home-made desserts make this neo-bistrot in a quiet corner of Paris a breath of fresh air.

ORIGINS 14

49 avenue Jean Moulin, 75014. +33 (0)1 45 45 68 58

www.origins14.com

Bistronomy pioneer La Régalade used to occupy this spot, now revamped and with a new chef at the helm, but with the same values of fresh produce cooked simply but well. For €37 per head you'll sample three courses, including the likes of chilled carrot and cardamom soup, pork fillet with roast beetroot and capers and roast damsons with buckwheat crumble.

LA CRÊPERIE DE JOSSELIN

67 rue du Montparnasse, 75014. +33 (0)1 43 20 93 50

On of the best of a crop of crêperies clustered around the Gare de Montparnasse – where trains arrive from Brittany, the home of the crêpe and its savoury sister the galette, made from a nutty and filling buckwheat batter called blé noir or sarrasin in French. There's often a queue for Josselin but you can pass the time as it snakes past the kitchen watching the chefs carve off butter in alarmingly large hunks to fry the enormous fresh galettes

and crêpes. Opt for one of the classic galettes such as ham, cheese and egg or something a bit different like the Finistère, with aubergine purée, egg and bacon. Just make sure you save room for a salted caramel crêpe for dessert and accompany the whole lot with a cup or two of dry cider.

Al Fresco Paris

LE PAVILLON MONTSOURIS

20 rue Gazan, 75014. +33 (0)1 43 13 29 00

www.pavillon-montsouris.com

Formal dining in one of Paris's loveliest parks in a restaurant built in 1889 in time for the 1892 Universal Exhibition and which is still going strong, giving city-fatigued Parisians a chance to breathe in the air and relax amid the greenery. A view like this – and soigné cuisine combining quality ingredients with a touch of innovation – doesn't come cheap: the set menu is €49.

Going Green

RAW CAKES

83 Rue Daguerre, 75014. +33 (0)9 86 12 73 48

https://www.facebook.com/ RawCakes-1263385443704818/

There's a pretty little haven of healthy eating on the market street of rue Daguerre where everything from burgers to lasagne, cupcakes to chia pudding is raw, vegan and gluten-free – but still delicious.

AUTO PASSION CAFÉ

197 boulevard Brune, 75014. +33 (0)1 45 43 20 20

www.autopassioncafe.fr

Proof that in a city as imaginative as Paris it's possible to find something for everyone comes in the form of this Formula 1-themed restaurant which even has a driving simulator. Definitely one for fans and long-suffering dining companions of fans, the menu, divided up into sections like a Formula 1 tournament (the grid, qualifiers etc) is actually decent – grilled fish and vegetables, sharing charcuterie platters and steaks galore but you're not really here for the food.

Café Culture

CAFÉ DAGUERRE

4 avenue du Général Leclerc, 75014. +33 (0)1 43 22 17 29

A traditional Parisian café complete with old-school zinc-topped bar. The outside tables are perfect for a spot of people-watching after a wander round the market.

HEXAGONE CAFÉ

121 rue du Château, 75014.
www.hexagone-cafe.fr

The team at Hexagone roast their own speciality coffees, making for a good-coffee oasis in a quiet part of the city.

Do It Yourself

ACCORDÉON PARIS GOURMANDS

80 rue Daguerre, 75014. +33 (0)1 43 21 74 49
www.accordeonparisgourmands.com

This unique shop is surely proof that Paris's gastronomic scene has everything – including an accordion and wine shop. Yes, an accordion and wine shop. An enterprising husband-and-wife team, sad to see that a local accordion shop had been closed for some years, decided to revive it, and opened up their quirky emporium in 2013 – accordions, a selection of French and a few Italian wines and spirits as well as a selection of gourmet delights such as nougat, jam, biscuits and pâté from the French regions. It's hard to imagine a more French shopping experience.

O SOLE MIO

44 rue Daguerre, 75014. +33 (0)1 43 22 88 28

It doesn't get more authentic than this Italian deli on the rue Daguerre, one of Paris's most pleasant market streets. Come for fine charcuterie and cheeses, fresh pasta and ready-made portions of your favourite Italian dishes.

FROMAGERIE VACROUX

5 rue Daguerre, 75014. +33 (0)1 43 22 09 04

Don't hesitate to ask for advice as you seek to navigate the frankly bewildering choice in this traditional cheesemonger – choose from comtés aged for different lengths of time or tell the friendly staff when you plan to eat your goat's cheese and whether you prefer it runny or more solid and they'll guide you.

Perfect Pâtisseries

DOMINIQUE SAIBRON

77 avenue du Général Leclerc, 75014. +33 (0)1 43 35 01 07
www.dominique-saibron.com

There's an astounding array of speciality bread at this popular pâtisserie-boulangerie – the seemingly permanent queue of locals outside tells you everything you need to know about the quality. Check out the chestnut bread or the fig and grain loaf if you're looking for something more original than the simple baguette – although that is a thing of beauty.

CHEZ BOGATO

7 rue Liancourt, 75014. +33 (0)140470351
www.chezbogato.fr

This beguiling cake shop and tea room is a testament to the imagination and creativity of its founder Anaïs Ohmer who left her job as an artistic director working in advertising to retrain as a pâtissier. Taking inspiration from the world of cupcakes and cookies as well as from more traditional desserts, she and her team work away in their lab-kitchen hybrid to come up with inventive delights including the Sweetburger (€39 to serve 4-6): macaron, chocolate ganache, raspberry and mint leaves disguised as a burger or the chocolate, strawberry marshmallow and mascarpone and

stracciatella mousse confection presented like a pizza. You can learn to make some of these fantastic creations yourself at workshops.

Cosmopolitan Paris

AYAKO-TEPPANYAKI

67 rue de l'Ouest, 75014. +33 (0)1 43 21 63 44
www.ayako.fr

Watch your food being cooked in front of you at this authentic Japanese teppanyaki grill.

UN JOUR A HA NOI

46 rue Daguerre, 75014. +33 (0)1 42 18 16 92

A tiny and cosy space thick with the fragrance of pho, the spicy lemongrassy noodle soup that is the house speciality.

18

15th Arrondissement

THIS QUIET RESIDENTIAL district has little to offer tourists in the way of sights but if you find yourself here, check out the bustling shopping street the rue du Commerce, the modern design of the huge parc André Citroën (on the site of the former Citroën car factory) complete with greenhouses and tethered balloon, the marché Grenelle market or the magnificent view from the Tour Montparnasse.

Pure Paris

LE CAFÉ DU COMMERCE
51 rue du Commerce, 75015. +33 (0)1 45 75 03 27
https://www.lecafeducommerce.com/la-carte/

All the brasserie stalwarts – seafood platters, prime cuts of Limousin beef, confit de canard – as well as a few surprises: le fish and chips, for example. The setting is lovely – with lush green foliage reaching up from the mosaic floor into an airy central atrium. On weekdays the main course and dessert menu with a coffee at €17.50 is well worth a try.

CIEL DE PARIS
33 avenue de Maine, 75015. +33 (0)1 40 64 77 64
www.cieldeparis.com

The Montparnasse tower, or Tour Maine Montparnasse to give it its official name, divides opinion like no other Parisian monument. The best many of the city's residents have to say about the hulking tower, finished in the early 1970s, is that when you're inside it, you can't see it, sticking one finger up to the Paris skyline. But even the building's harshest critic would have to admit that the view from Ciel de Paris, on the fifty-sixth floor, across the grey rooftops to the Eiffel Tower in the west and the Sacré Cœur in the north, is spectacular. Chef Christophe Marchais, with his work cut out distracting diners from the panorama, opts for punchy flavour combinations such as a starter of crab and scallops with seaweed, yuzu cream and a mango and passion fruit dressing (€28) or a rich main course of veal fillet and sweetbreads, foie gras and truffle (€44). The three-course Menu Grand Écran including drinks at €136 is a good option or just enjoy the view with a glass of champagne or a cocktail in the bar.

BRASSERIE LOLA

99 rue du Théâtre, 75015. +33 (0)1 45 78 22 35

http://brasserie-lola.business.site

Cocktails and simple French cuisine based on seasonal ingredients – and in a nod to the location's former incarnation as a vegan restaurant, the new owners have made sure to keep some vegetarian and vegan dishes on the menu.

LA VILLA CORSE

164 boulevard de Grenelle, 75015. +33 (0)1 53 86 70 81

www.lavillacorse.com

Specialities from Corsica made with ingredients sourced from the best producers and served with flair in a chic setting. Try the cannelloni stuffed with local cheese, brocciu, and artichoke (€21).

Best Bistrots

LE TROQUET

21 rue François Bonvin, 75015. +33 (0)1 34 66 89 00

www.restaurantletroquet.fr

This buzzing place is just how a Parisian bistrot should be with tables crammed into a warm and welcoming space, harried-but-friendly staff and a constantly changing chalkboard menu full of simple but perfectly executed dishes designed to let the ingredients do the talking.

L'OS À MOELLE

3 rue Vasco de Gama, 75015. +33 (0)1 45 57 27 27

www.osamoelle-restaurant.com

L'Os à Moelle means bone marrow, which gives an indication of the meaty priorities of this high-class bistronomic address in the quiet 15th arrondissement. You can try the bone marrow itself (€8) or go for a starter of pigs' trotter terrine with Puy lentils (€9) or a main course of suckling pig fricassée. In short, not one for vegetarians. La Cave de l'Os à Moelle is nearby (at 181 rue de Lourmel, also in the 15th).

L'ACCOLADE

208 rue de la Croix Nivert, 75015. +33 (0)1 45 57 73 20

https://www.laccoladeparis.fr

Big industrial ceiling lamps and wide windows give a spacious feel to this neighbourhood bistrot where you'll find a short and regularly changing menu full of classic dishes with an inspired twist. The evening menu of three courses plus cheese at €35 is great value for money.

Pop-Up Paris

CHAT MALLOWS CAFÉ

30 rue des Volontaires, 75015.

www.chatmallowscafe.fr

One for feline fans as this is Paris's very own cat café – the space is set up for the furry inhabitants who prowl around or sleep curled up in cosy corners. There's a simple menu of sweet and savoury snacks and hot and cold drinks. Booking required (via the website).

Café Culture

O COFFEESHOP
23 rue de Lourmel, 75015.
www.ocoffeeshop.com

The Australian coffee revolution has reached the 15th, with brilliant blends and even Lamingtons to go with them.

CAFÉ BEAUGRENELLE
89 rue Saint-Charles, 75015. +33 (0)1 45 77 72 21
http://cafebeaugrenelle.fr

You'll get a better cup of coffee in the more hipsterish Australian-style brunch-and-coffee shops springing up all over Paris but it's hard to beat this big terrace for a spot of people-watching.

Do It Yourself

MARCHÉ GRENELLE
boulevard de Grenelle, 75015. +33 (0)1 45 11 71 11
http://equipement.paris.fr/marche-grenelle-5502

On Wednesday and Sunday mornings this stretch of the boulevard fills up with stands selling cheese, bread, flowers, fruit and veg as well as speciality products from the regions.

Helen Massy-Beresford

OLIVIERS & CO
85 rue du Commerce, 75015. +33 (0)1 55 76 42 26
https://www.oliviers-co.com/fr/

A dizzying array of olive oils and olive oil-based delicacies as well as crackers and biscuits, vinegars and conserves. Everything you need for an apéro à la française.

FROMAGERIE LAURENT DUBOIS
2 rue de Lourmel, 75015. +33 (0)1 45 78 70 58
http://www.fromageslaurentdubois.fr/fr/

An unbelievable selection of top quality artisan cheeses from across France and all its many and varied cheese-making regions, plus a few from further afield too.

Perfect Pâtisseries

SADAHARU AOKI
25 rue Pérignon, 75015. +33 (0)1 43 06 02 71
www.sadaharuaoki.com

Tokyo-born pastry chef Sadaharu Aoki brings together Japanese flavours

Matcha éclair at Sadaharu Aoki. Jean-Charles Karmann

– think matcha, red bean paste and sesame – with the traditional techniques and aesthetics of French pâtisserie in a gloriously delicate feast for the eyes and the tastebuds. Try the black sesame éclair or the Ginza, a jaunty striped creation that bears a passing resemblance to a traditional fraisier but marries hibiscus cream with redcurrants, raspberries and strawberries on an almond biscuit base. There are branches in the 5th, 6th and 7th arrondissements as well as a stand at Lafayette Gourmet in the 9th.

DES GÂTEAUX ET DU PAIN – CLAIRE DAMON

63 boulevard Pasteur, 75015. 06 98 95 33 18
www.desgateauxetdupain.com

The sober matte black interiors in one of Claire Damon's two Paris boutiques (the other is in the 7th at 89 rue Bac) perfectly sets off the delicate designs of the cakes and tarts that have revealed her extraordinary originality and creative flair. Try the Kashmir (€6.60) – marrying exotic aromas

of saffron, dates and orange
fragrant Pamplemousse Ros
brings together rose and grapefruit in a petal-strewn whole.

POÎLANE

49 Boulevard de Grenelle, 75015.
www.poilane.com

Home of the famous Poîlane sourdough loaf.

Cosmopolitan Paris

LE CONCERT DE CUISINE

14 rue Nélaton, 75015. +33 (0)1 40 58 10 15

High-end fusion – Japanese teppanyaki meets French cuisine in an elegant pared back dining room with a short but satisfying menu.

CO TU

24 rue de la Croix Nivert, 75015. +33 (0)1 42 73 20 42
https://www.facebook.com/CoTu2.0/

Great little Vietnamese place where you can fill up on all the classics: crispy nems, fragrant soups, crunchy bo bun or sweet caramelized pork.

LES DÉLICES DU MAROC

18 rue Frémicourt, 75015. +33 (0)1 45 75 51 81
https://restaurant-les-delices-du-maroc-moroccan-restaurant.business.site

Excellent cous cous as well as tajines, pastillas and more at this friendly and welcoming Moroccan restaurant.

19

16th Arrondissement

THE 16TH IS ONE of the city's richest areas, and it shows – with its grand boulevards, opulent hotels and general aura of wealth on every corner. It's also home to the verdant expanse of the Bois de Boulogne and some world-class museums, including the Asian art specialist the Musée Guimet, the anthropology museum the Musée de l'Homme and the wonderful Monet-focused Musée Marmottan, where the setting, in a beautifully preserved old hôtel particulier, sets the works on display off to perfection. Although the casual vibe gradually taking over the rest of Paris's dining scene is mostly lacking here, the 16th is still home to some gastronomic gems.

Pure Paris

MASHA

85 avenue Kléber, 75016. +33 (0)1 42 25 98 85

www.masha-paris.com

Street art and fashion photography combine with high-end French gastronomy and a talented Japanese chef in this new opening in the chic 16th arrondissement.

Masha

Masha

COMICE

31 avenue de Versailles, 75016. +33 (0)1 42 15 55 70

https://comice.paris

Husband and wife – chef and sommelier – team Noam Gedalof and Etheliya Hananova bring their combined thirty years of experience in the restaurant business in California, New York and

Greek yoghurt pannacotta with olive oil, yuzu and orange blossom at Comice
Marie Hennechart

Montreal to bear at this Michelin-starred establishment in one of Paris's chicest corners. There's a three-course lunch menu for €46 or the €80 per head option (or €120 in the evening) including four or

Comice interior. Marie Hennechart

five courses plus wine adapted to your requirements and the chef's specialities of the moment.

Best Bistrots

LE PETIT PERGOLÈSE

38 rue Pergolèse, 75016. +33 (0)1 45 00 23 66
A quirkily-decorated neighbourhood bistrot offering top quality cuisine. Starters begin at around €14 and main courses at about €26 with desserts coming in around the €15 mark – not too expensive for the neighbourhood.

LE BRANDEVIN

29 rue du Dr Blanche, 75016. +33 (0)1 42 24 19 33
www.lebrandevin.fr

A great traditional French bistrot, with classic dishes, quality ingredients and a warm welcome.

LA CAUSERIE
31 rue Vital, 75016. +33 (0)1 45 20 33 00
www.lacauserie.fr

Three courses for €36 at this welcoming bistrot, where fresh and seasonal ingredients are crafted into the best of French regional cooking with a modern twist.

Oeuf meurette. La Causerie

La Causerie. La Causerie

Al Fresco Paris

LE CHALET DES ÎLES
Lac inférieur du Bois de Boulogne, porte de la Muette, 75016. +33 (0)1 42 88 04 69
http://chalet-des-îles.com

It doesn't get greener than this classy restaurant set on an island in a lake in the bucolic Bois de Boulogne. The vast terrace looking out over the water is perfect for a break from the built-up city on a sunny day.

LA GRANDE CASCADE
allée de Longchamp, bois de Boulogne, 75016. +33 (0)1 45 27 33 51

If you prefer your fix of greenery with a more opulent backdrop, this Michelin-starred fine dining establishment led by chef Frédéric Robert, which is also in the Bois de Boulogne, is for you. With starters from around €65 and fixed menus starting from €109, a picnic in the woods may be a more economic option, however.

The terrace at L'Oiseau Blanc. L'Oiseau Blanc

L'OISEAU BLANC

19 avenue Kléber, 75016. +33 (0)1 58 12
67 30

www.paris.peninsula.com

The view from the rooftop terrace of the
restaurant at The Peninsula Hotel is pure
magic and the upmarket menu is divine
too. Set deals start at €69 per person or
in spring, why not try the €165 asparagus
menu – a tour de force of five courses
specifically designed to showcase this
prized ingredient.

LE PRÉ CATELAN

Bois de Boulogne, 75016. +33 (0)1 44 14
41 14

http://restaurant.leprecatelan.com

The bucolic setting and ostentatious
décor of this Michelin-starred
restaurant are impressive, but the
cuisine itself – and its presentation
– are out of this world: Chef Frédéric
Anton conjures up culinary magic in the
form of delicate, intensely flavoured and
beautifully put together morsels which
you can try for €130 a head for a four-
course lunch menu.

Le Pré Catelan. Richard Haughton

Pop-Up Paris

BUSTRONOME
2 avenue Kléber, 75016.
+33 (0)9 54 44 45 55
www.bustronome.com

Enjoy a three-course meal with a panoramic view of some of the city's most famous sights – from the comfort of a specially fitted-out double-decker bus. Lunch is €65 a head or €85 with wine so it's not cheap but it's certainly original.

Café Culture

LE COFFEE PARISIEN
7 rue Gustave Courbet, 75016. +33 (0)1 45 53 17 17.

American meets French at this brunch spot in the 16th. There's another branch in the 6th at 4 rue Princesse as well as Coffee Club at 87 rue d'Assas, also in the 6th.

LA ROTONDE DE LA MUETTE
12 chaussée de la Muette, 75016. +33 (0)1 45 24 45 45
http://www.rotondemuette.paris

There's a classy bistrot menu at this gilded and opulent neighbourhood institution. Or it's just as nice to sit on the spacious terrace and sip a drink as you watch the world go by.

Do It Yourself

DELIZIUS
40 rue de l'Annonciation, 75016. +33 (0)1 42 88 07 08
https://www.facebook.com/DeliziusTraiteur/

You'll find everything you need for an Italian feast at home at this upmarket deli: fresh and dried pasta, Parma ham, grilled aubergines and peppers, mozzarella and a good selection of Italian wines. There are branches in the 5th (134 rue Mouffetard) and 17th (30 rue des Moines) too.

LA GRANDE ÉPICERIE
80 rue de Passy, 75016.
www.lagrandepicerie.com

A smaller outpost of the main event in the 7th at 38 rue de Sèvres, this upmarket deli and grocery store is nonetheless a treasure trove of gourmet goodies.

FAYE PARIS
76 avenue Paul Doumer, 75016. +33 (0)1 40 72 01 01
www.faye-gastronomie.com

This supplier to many of Paris's top chefs opened up its retail boutique in 2002 giving customers access to shelves groaning with top quality oil, vinegar, wine, preserves, pâté and truffles and mushrooms – the speciality.

Perfect Pâtisseries

LA PÂTISSERIE CYRIL LIGNAC
2 rue de Chaillot, 75016.
www.gourmand-croquant.com

The bold designs and exquisite flavours

Charlotte Lindet

of Cyril Lignac's creations have ensured him a place among the stars of French pâtisserie. The original – and slightly alarming – red-spotted exterior of the Equinoxe hides a delicious concoction of bourbon vanilla cream, salted butter caramel and speculoos biscuit. This branch offers the whole range of pâtisserie, chocolate, bread and macarons and there are other branches dotted across the capital.

Cosmopolitan Paris

SHANG PALACE
10 avenue d'Iéna, 75016. +33 (0)1 5367 1992
http://www.shangri-la.com/paris/shangrila/dining/restaurants/shang-palace/

Exceptional Cantonese cuisine – it became the only Chinese restaurant in France to be awarded a Michelin star in 2012 – in as sumptuous a setting as you would imagine from the Shangri-La hotel.

FUXIA
91 avenue Raymond-Poincaré, 75016. +33 (0)1 45 00 46 80
www.fuxia-cantina.fr

A casual Italian eatery where the emphasis is on hearty dishes done well – there are few surprises among the pasta, risotto, salads and sharing charcuterie platters but the quality is high and with numerous branches dotted across Paris, its suburbs and in other French cities, Fuxia is a good go-to Italian option and especially a rare reasonably priced and relaxed spot in an expensive district.

LILI
19 avenue Kléber, 75016. +33 (0)1 58 12 67 50.

This Cantonese restaurant inside the Peninsula hotel is exquisite on every level: the space, the service and of course the signature dim sum. There's a €58 lunch menu.

Wok fried blue lobster with ginger and spring onions. Lili

17th Arrondissement

THE 17TH IS A diverse arrondissement, with large staid Haussmannian boulevards in the south-western part closest to the parc Monceau (which itself is in the 8th) and the more rough-and-ready parts towards the north of the district. The highlight is the lively but increasingly upmarket area that is Batignolles, packed with little cafés, bars, restaurants and boutiques as well as a great covered market, centred around the pretty Sainte Marie de Batignolles church and close to the charmingly leafy Square des Batignolles.

Pure Paris

CHEZ GEORGES

273 boulevard Péreire, 75017. +33 (0)1 45 74 31 00

http://www.restaurantsparisiens.com/chez-georges/contact/

It doesn't get much more traditional than Chez Georges, a dark-wooded haven of starched linen, discreet but efficient service and old-fashioned food – veal's head, roast pigeon and kidneys all feature on the throw-back menu.

LE REFUGE DES MOINES

85 rue des Moines, 75107. +33 (0)1 42 28 92 52

www.baravinlerefugedesmoines.com

Tuck into the best of what France's diverse regions have to offer at this charmingly old-fashioned bistrot and wine bar. With an extensive and eclectic wine list and restaurant choices including the likes of foie gras with Calvados-caramelised apples (€26), south-west style duck breast with black cherry sauce (€26) or Provençal style king prawns (€30) to choose from, make sure you've worked up a good appetite.

Best Bistrots

LE BOUCHON ET L'ASSIETTE

127 rue Cardinet, 75017. +33 (0)1 42 27 83 93

Fresh seasonal dishes with Basque accents make this a top gourmet stop. It's tucked a few minutes' walk away from the centre of the Batignolles area but it's popular so wise to call ahead. Try the homemade basque cake for dessert, served with a pineapple 'minestrone'.

CRÊPE COEUR

66 rue des Dames, 75017. +33 (0)1 43 87 35 99

Come for a taste of Brittany – savoury

buckwheat galettes and sweet crêpes as well as artisan cider – in this pared-back little crêperie in the heart of the trendy and lively Batignolles district.

LE P'TIT MUSSET

132 rue Cardinet, 75017. +33 (0)1 42 27 36 78
http://leptitmusset.fr/en

With Le Bouchon et l'Assiette across the road this little stretch of the rather nondescript rue Cardinet is in danger of becoming a gourmet hotspot. Like its opposite neighbour, Le P'tit Musset places the emphasis on fresh seasonal ingredients combined into inventive dishes, all served up in an airy dining room, all blond wood and blue walls. Charming and good value with three courses for €35. For a more casual bite there are charcuterie and cheese platters that go perfectly with happy hour aperitifs.

L'ENVIE DU JOUR

106 rue Nollet, 75017. +33 (0)1 42 26 01 02.
www.lenviedujour.com

What it lacks in choice, L'Envie du Jour makes up for in flavour and presentation. Of course, the limited menu options are deliberate, with two choices for each course changing daily to showcase the seasonal ingredients and the chefs' ingenuity. The mint green walls and simple décor lend the place a relaxed vibe. The 'menu découverte' (discovery menu) offers a taster portion of two starters, two main courses and two

desserts for €44. L'Envie du Jour offers Sunday brunches as well as cookery courses too.

Al Fresco Paris

LE BISTROT DES DAMES

18 rue des Dames, 75017. +33 (0)1 45 22 13 42
www.eldoradohotel.fr

This little bistrot is a true hidden gem with tables in a quiet leafy courtyard where you can choose from a large selection of good quality wines or dine on homemade French classics.

TERRASSE 17

17 rue des Batignolles, 75017. +33 (0)1 43 87 77 80
www.terrasse17.com

Good quality brasserie classics, salads and tartines (open sandwiches) all with a lovely shady terrace seating area in the heart of the lively Batignolles district.

Going Green

LITTLE NONNA

12 avenue Niel, 75017. +33 (0)1 46 22 68 17.
www.littlenonnaparis.com

Launching a gluten-free pizzeria in the city of the baguette was perhaps a risky move, but for the team behind Little Nonna it appears to be paying off. The menu offers a good selection of pizzas in two sizes and individual pasta dishes or vast bowls to share as well as antipasti,

Gluten free pasta and pizza at Little Nonna. Little Nonna.

salads and sharing platters. The gluten-free pizza made from a blend of corn, rice and buckwheat flours is a highlight while the pasta dishes are good too.

MACA'RONG

175 rue Legendre, 75017. +33 (0)9 53 65 64 84
**https://www.facebook.com/
macaroncosy/**

A tempting selection of gluten-free, sugar-free (made using maltitol) and vegan macarons, cup cakes and other sweet treats in this little tea salon, where there are regular workshops so you can learn how to make them yourself.

SUPER VEGAN

118 rue des Moines, 75017. +33 (0)9 51 56 99 16
www.supervegan.fr

Here to save the day for all hungry vegans in France – it's Super Vegan! Thankfully no Lycra-clad superheros here, just a commitment from the founders to prove that it's possible to eat heartily and well and at a reasonable price without consuming animal products. To prove their point, while there's a varied menu of burgers, salads and desserts, the house speciality is the Super Kebab, at €6, a filling bite of seitan (wheat gluten) kebab with salad and homemade sauce with vegan cheese (the wonderfully named fauxmage) €1 extra.

Pop-Up Paris

MYLO CONCEPT STORE

61 rue Legendre, 75017. +33 (0)1 42 47 16 15.
**https://www.facebook.com/Mylo.
ConceptStore/**

Half of this pretty pastel-hued store is

given over to clothes and accessories from chic French brands such as Les Petits Hauts and Bazar Exquis, while the little restaurant corner offers healthy light meals: think butternut squash soup, avocado toast, cold-pressed juices and gluten-free cakes and cookies.

LE COSTAUD DES BATIGNOLLES

10 rue Brochant, 75017. 06 82 82 89 82
http://www.lecostaud.fr

Get your art fix while you lunch at this gallery-restaurant in the buzzing Batignolles quarter.

Café Culture

DOSE

82 place du Dr Félix Lobligeois, 75017.
www.dosedealercafe.fr

Dose, which subtitles itself your 'coffee dealer' is the place to be for a great flat white or matcha latte, fresh juices, wholegrain baguette sandwiches, brownies, cookies and cakes. There's another branch at 73 rue Mouffetard in the 5th, while the trendy-but-cosy industrial-style décor is just the thing in Batignolles, this bobo corner of the 17th.

LE MONCEAU

4 avenue de Villiers, 75017. +33 (0)1 43 87 28 34

There's a brasserie-style menu or you can simply sip a coffee or a glass of wine and watch the comings and goings from the terrace.

Do It Yourself

MAISON CASTRO

47 rue des Moines, 75017. +33 (0)1 53 11 08 57.
www.maisoncastro.com

For a lunchtime sandwich, Maison Castro is a much more inviting prospect than the often rather samey boulangerie offerings. Crunchy baguettes with generous and original fillings including chorizo, artichoke cream, tomato and rocket, a daily changing pasta dish and top-notch deli items too. Perfect for a picnic and there are also branches in the 9th, 10th and 20th arrondissements.

AU BOUT DU CHAMP

20 rue des Dames, 75017.
https://www.auboutduchamp.com

Forget plastic-wrapped supermarket offerings, at Au Bout Du Champ you can pick up freshly picked seasonal fruit and vegetables, often organic, from small-scale producers less than 100km away. There are also artisan honeys, jams and soups as well as free-range eggs. The knowledgeable staff will give you recipe ideas for some of the more obscure produce too. There's another branch in the 18th at 118 rue Caulaincourt.

L'ATRYUM DES SAVEURS

80 rue de Tocqueville, 75017. +33 (0)1 47 64 01 30
www.atryum.com

A veritable smorgasbord of top-notch mezze-style food from across the Mediterranean: smoked aubergines, salt

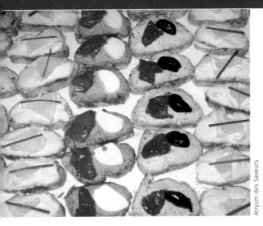

Atryum des Saveurs

cod, hummus, spanakopita, moussaka, grilled skewers.

MARCHÉ COUVERT BATIGNOLLES
96bis rue Lemercier, 75017 01 48 85 93 30

This covered market has a bit of everything, fruit and veg, cheese, wine, roast chickens, Lebanese and Moroccan food stands. And it's situated in the heart of a great food shopping area too so if you don't find what you're looking for here there's plenty of choice in the neighbouring streets.

Perfect Pâtisseries

ACIDE MACARON
24 rue des Moines, 75017. +33 (0)1 42 61 60 61
www.acidemacaron.com

A modern take on traditional French pâtisserie at this concept store which offers breakfast, brunch and lunch options as well as cutting edge versions of pâtisserie favourites and imaginatively flavoured macarons such as green tea and jasmine, bubble gum or poppy seed and coconut milk.

LA ROMAINVILLE
23 rue des Moines, 75017. +33 (0)1
www.laromainville.fr

Cakes, tarts and desserts made with creativity and flair probably explain why this neighbourhood pâtisserie has been in business for 70 years. Check out the tiramisu safari – a leopard-print version of the classic Italian dessert.

Cosmopolitan Paris

HARPERS
31 rue Legendre, 75017. +33 (0)1 42 67 15 45
http://www.harpers-restaurant.com

Gourmet burgers Paris-style, bistrot classics, salads and sandwiches. There's another branch in the 18th at 16 rue Letort.

LIBERIC
95 rue Lemercier, 75017. +33 (0)6 64 33 03 89
https://www.facebook.com/libericparis/

Live music and tasty tapas go hand in hand in this little Spanish bodega.

MAISON ANAME
101 rue Nollet, 75017. +33 (0)1 42 29 72 46.
www.aname.fr

This Vietnamese restaurant proudly proclaims everything is homemade, except for the Nutella used in the sweet banh cuon crêpes and there's no MSG either. Don't miss the homemade nems (spring rolls) served the Vietnamese way, wrapping them in lettuce and fresh mint leaves before dipping in fish sauce.

Helen Massy-Beresford

Cookery class at Maison Aname.

Of the main dishes, the caramel pork (€14.50) is a winner as is the bo bun which chef and owner Ange Hong Lan explains is not such a popular dish in Vietnam as it is in France – don't let that stop you. Maison Aname also offers weekend cooking workshops for children and adults.

MAMMA ROMA

98 avenue Niel, 75017. +33 (0)9 86 42 30 28

Good quality pizza al taglio (by the slice) just like in Rome. Perfect for an on-the-go snack. There are other branches across Paris.

MÉNÉLIK

4 rue Sauffroy, 75017. +33 (0)1 46 27 00 82
www.menelikrestaurant.com

Try spicy and varied Ethiopian curries all served on injera pancakes – which are used as cutlery too – at this lively little restaurant. On Fridays and Saturdays there's a traditional Ethiopian tea ceremony.

21

18th Arrondissement

THE 18TH IS A district of contrasts: most obviously between the postcard-perfect cobbled streets of Montmartre and the nearby Pigalle district where the legendary cabarets of the Moulin Rouge era have given way to seedier sex shops. There's the contrast between some of the last working-class – albeit rapidly gentrifying – areas of Paris and the tourist hotspots: the marché aux puces de St-Ouen (Clignancourt flea market – Europe's largest, which is actually just outside the city limits) attracts thousands of visitors at the weekends and the few hundred square metres of Montmartre surrounding the Sacré Cœur are among the most visited on the planet. It's often better to step outside those tourist-thronged streets for a good value lunch or dinner. A few minutes' walk away you could be in a different world: the African market stalls and shops around the rue Dejean selling bissap and plantain as well as a wonderfully exotic selection of fruits and vegetables, restaurants serving up spicy peanut sauce (mafé) from Senegal in the Goutte d'Or district, home to a significant West African population following decades of immigration from France's former colonies or the vast choice of Indian and Sri Lankan restaurants in the streets around La Chapelle.

Pure Paris

CAFÉ FRANCŒUR
129 rue Caulaincourt, 75018, Paris.
+33 (0)1 53 28 00 15

This welcoming brasserie-style restaurant is open 365 days a year – even on Christmas Day it's buzzing with regulars enjoying the likes of oysters, chestnut soup, roast chicken, a wide variety of steaks including a 1.2 kg côte de bœuf to share at €67, as well as hearty salads and homemade desserts. Service is friendly and efficient with English-speaking staff.

Helen Massy-Beresford

BRASSERIE BARBÈS

2 boulevard Barbès, 75018. +33 (0)1 42 64 52 23

www.brasseriebarbes.com

A recent addition to Paris's brasserie scene, Brasserie Barbès is a clear sign of the gentrification taking place in the 18th arrondissement, with its white walls and striped awnings a stark contrast with the scruffy boulevard it calls home. The menu includes typical brasserie fare with original touches and Spanish accents – think spicy Basque sausage with padrón peppers at €17 or sole meunière with tarragon-infused mash for €33. The weekend brunch deal is good value at €18, based around eggs benedict with a selection of side dishes and finished off with chocolate and banana pancakes and there's a lovely rooftop terrace.

Best Bistrots

CHEZ FOUCHER MÈRE ET FILLE

13 rue Madeline Réberioux, 75018. +33 (0)9 54 33 16 66.

https://www.chezfoucherparis.com

Short of getting yourself adopted into a French family, this is probably the next best way to get a taste of real French home cooking, with homely classics such as sausages with lentils or quiche lorraine plus a tempting array of homemade cakes. Lunch is served up on mismatched plates while the two resident dogs cruise the room in search of leftovers. It's a little out of the way but worth the twenty-minute walk

from touristy Montmartre. The mother and daughter team work closely with producers and insist on using as many local ingredients as they can – their ham is from Paris and vegetables come from the wider Île de France region, for example. Service is canteen-style and at lunchtimes it is packed with local office workers.

PATAKREP

89 rue Duhesme, 75018. +33 (0)9

Traditional Breton buckwheat savoury galettes as well as sweet pancakes and charcuterie and cheese platters for apéro time, all served in a school-themed space: there are desks and other school furniture, the menu looks like an exercise book and in keeping with the aesthetic, it's genuinely child-friendly, with a little selection of toys and books for younger diners.

LES ROUTIERS

50bis rue Marx Dormoy, 75018. +33 (0)1 46 07 93 80.

Come for a slice of old-school traditional French country cuisine (although not specific to any one region) – andouillette sausage, rillettes, kidneys, braised lamb or rabbit will give you a taste of France outside the Paris city walls and a world away from the hipster coffee houses and neo-bistros springing up in this fast-changing corner of the 18th. The ambience is old-school as well and from the outside the restaurant looks extremely unpromising, but as one of the last 'routier' eateries aimed at hungry but discerning truck drivers, it's in demand and often full.

POLISSONS

35 rue Ramey, 75018. 06 46 63 57 50
**https://www.facebook.com/www.
polissons.restaurant.fr/**

Clean lines and polished hardwood give a Scandinavian feel to this modern bistro, where you can watch the chef hard at work in the open kitchen, putting together inventive dishes such as a starter of egg yolk ravioli with roast ham (€10) or a main course of pork with horseradish (€19) or go for the constantly changing fish of the day.

Les Trois Frères. Helen Massy-Beresford

Asparagus and soft boiled egg at Polissons.
Helen Massy-Beresford

LES TROIS FRÈRES

14 rue Léon, 75018. +33 (0)1 42 64 91 73.

You could easily miss Les Trois Frères, tucked away as it is on an unprepossessing street in the heart of the Goutte d'Or district. It's a cosy and unpretentious neighbourhood bistrot with a good value menu of home-made classics such as Toulouse sausage with lentils for €10, cous-cous for €11.50 and chocolate mousse for €3.50. Service is charming and décor is eccentric – a favourite with locals.

BOUILLON PIGALLE

22 boulevard de Clichy, 75018. +33 (0)1 42 59 69 31
**http://www.bouillonpigalle.com
https://www.facebook.com/
BouillonPigalle/**

The traditional Bouillon – a cheap and cheerful place for Parisians of all budgets to tuck into the likes of frisée salad with lardons or bœuf bourguignon – may be all but extinct (see Bouillon Chartier in the 9th arrondissement for one survivor). But the team behind Bouillon Pigalle has breathed new life into the concept (the name refers back to the signature dish of beef in its own stock or bouillon served in the original Bouillon which catered to the Les Halles market workers). The team behind Bouillon Pigalle has kept some traditional elements but draping foliage and an artful smattering of vintage posters bring the décor bang up to date. On the menu are the classics Parisians expect from a bouillon and somewhat surprisingly the prices are traditionally low too: eggs mayonnaise at €1.90, herrings at €4.50, main courses of sausage and mash at €11.50 or blanquette de veau at €10.50.

CAFÉ MIROIR

94 rue des Martyrs, 75018. +33 (0)1 46 06 50 73
http://www.cafemiroir.com

French bistrot classics cooked with care and good ingredients in a friendly setting – this is a great option in touristy Montmartre.

FICHON

98 rue Marcadet, 75018. +33 (0)9 70 94 52 14
www.fichon.fr

Fichon styles itself as a cave à poissons or 'fish cellar' – a convivial and airy space where you can choose from an extensive range of wines by the bottle or glass as well as excellent cocktails, all selected to perfectly complement the delicate and creative fish and seafood dishes on the menu. Don't hesitate to ask the friendly staff to guide you. There are small tapas-style plates as well as a full menu, with a typical main course at €21 pairing scallops with cress, ricotta, granny smith apple and dried black olives.

CHEZ FRANCIS LA BUTTE

122 rue Caulaincourt, 75018, Paris. +33 (0)1 42 23 58 26.

Head to this casual, friendly bar/restaurant when it's sunny for its large terrace, ideal for watching the world go by and it's not far from the heart of Montmartre, accessed by the staircase just outside the café. On a grey Parisian day the vibrant yellow colour scheme – not to mention the homemade chips and great apéro deals – will cheer you up.

LE LAMARCK

8 rue Lamarck, 75018.
www.lelamarck.fr

A tiny but good quality neo-bistrot just a few steps from the Sacré Coeur but somehow slightly off the tourist track – a short, regularly changing menu offers the likes of prawn, pesto and filo parcels (€16.50) or Puglia burrata with roast hazelnuts and butternut squash cream (€16.50) cooked well, with friendly English-speaking service and an original wine list to match.

Moimem

LA VIEILLE PIE
24 rue Pajol, 75018. +33 (0)9 83 39 04 39.
http://lavieillepie.com

Great burgers and home made skin-on
chips are the order of the day at this
unpretentious café where the service is
friendly. At weekends you can choose
between American, English and French-
style brunch deals and the relaxed coffee
shop by day transforms into a lively bar
at night.

LA RECYCLERIE
83 boulevard Ornano, 75018 01 42 57 58 49
www.larecyclerie.com

Good value weekend brunch deals (€22)
and homemade local, often vegetarian
food are the order of the day at this
urban farm. A long thin strip of land
containing chicken coops and vegetable
plots unfurls alongside the side of an
abandoned railway line at the edge of
the 18th arrondissement. A bottle of
the homemade lemonade is perfect

La REcyclerie

La REcyclerie.

on a sunny day, sipped in a rare corner of green in this dense part of Paris. La REcyclerie offers a packed calendar of workshops with a social conscience – think yoga, naturopathy and how to consume less, while you can bring your faulty appliances to the onsite repair shop for a new lease of life. Even the food waste from the café gets recycled to feed the animals on the farm.

KIEZ BIERGARTEN
Kiez Biergarten, 24 rue Vauvenargues, 75018. +33 (0)1 46 27 78 46
www.kiez.fr

The garden of Kiez Biergarten in the 18th arrondissement is tiny but if you can squeeze onto a table for weissbier and a pretzel it's a real haven. There's also a branch on the Bassin de la Villette in the 19th – Kiez Kanal.

MUSÉE DE MONTMARTRE – JARDINS RENOIR
12 rue Cortot, 75018. +33 (0)1 49 25 89 39
www.museedemontmartre.fr

Visit the small but informative museum housed in the oldest building in Montmartre to learn more about how this once-rural spot became a bohemian haven for artists and cabaret performers. Montmartre used to be a patchwork of vineyards and you can look out from the shady lawns of the museum gardens – its real draw – on to the last remaining plot of Montmartre vines. The grapes are still made into a wine that forms the focal point of a local celebration every year.

The gardens of the Musée de Montmartre. Helen Massy-Beresford

Montmartre's vineyard.
Helen Massy-Beresford.

The musuem's Café Renoir (named after the artist Auguste Renoir who lived here) won't win any prizes for gastronomy but for a quick coffee-and-cake stop in the tranquil garden the location is hard to beat.

Going Green

L'ABATTOIR VÉGÉTAL
61 rue Ramey, 75018.
https://www.facebook.com/abattoirvegetal/

Intricate, flavourful and imaginative vegetarian dishes, many of which are vegan too, in an instagrammable setting, all cascading plants and rose gold fittings – it's no wonder this new venue in the up-and-coming 18th is popular. The three-course set menu at €18 is excellent value, as is the €25 weekend brunch.

LE TRÈS PARTICULIER
23 avenue Junot, Pavillon D, 75018.
https://en.hotel-particulier-montmartre.com/bar

This bar may be one of Paris's loveliest spots – a verdant little space perfect for sipping a cocktail, tucked away within the Hôtel Particulier Montmartre.

Pop-Up Paris

LORD OF BARBÈS GIN
64 rue de Clignancourt, 75018. 06 87 22 81 21
www.lordofbarbesgin.com

The self-styled Lord of Barbès (the area around Barbès-Rochechouart metro

Helen Massy-Beresford

Lord of Barbès gin

station) is a true eccentric and has channelled his creativity into a top-class gin, distilled in small batches using original botanicals – juniper of course but also baobab, mango, coriander and cardamom – and presented in a stunning blue bottle embossed with a skull and cross bones. While you can taste the gin in numerous bars in the area it's worth a stop at the eccentric boutique to buy a bottle (€59 for 500mls) or simply to chat to the 'Lord' himself about his creation and check out the décor – old dolls in bell jars, skeletons and religious icons.

LE BAL CAFÉ OTTO

6 impasse de la Défense, 75018. +33 (0)1 44 70 75 51

http://www.le-bal.fr/le-bal-cafe-x-otto

The Viennese vibe at the café of this photography-focused exhibition space is the work of Austrian chef Lisa Machian but her cuisine is not limited to her home country – spicy accents and ingredients from around the world liven up dishes like dumplings stuffed with pork, pine nuts and sumac or wiener schnitezel with cranberry jam and aïoli. Come for brunch, lunch or tapas-style light bites in the evening. It's tucked away down an alley and looks out onto a little green park – a rare peaceful terrace in this built-up corner of Paris – and regularly hosts pop-up events and visiting chefs.

Rösti brunch: Café Otto at Le Bal. Helen Massy-Beresford

Café Culture

CAFÉ PIMPIN

64 rue Ramey, 75018, Paris. +33 (0)1 46 06 97 25

https://www.facebook.com/Café-Pimpin-1843551375882237/

'Good coffee and easy food' proclaims the menu and it's a pretty fair summary of this pared back café. Find space on one of the sunny trestle tables outside in summer to enjoy tasty and healthy salads, toasties, fresh juices, excellent Café Lomi coffee and delicious cookies, cakes and scones. Homesick Brits will also take comfort from the giant jar of Marmite available to adorn sourdough toast at breakfast time.

CAFÉ LOMI

3ter rue Marcadet, 75018. +33 (0)9 80 39 56 24

https://lomi.paris

The co-founder of this café-roastery-coffee school was horrified by the quality of the coffee he found in France when he moved here from Australia so decided to do something about it. Lomi was at the vanguard of a wave of speciality coffee places that is engulfing Paris, chasing away weak cups of robusta and replacing them with something infinitely better. There's the café itself – a relaxed space with an industrial feel and invariably many remote workers on laptops – where you can savour anything from a simple filter coffee to an espresso paired with blue cheese if you're feeling adventurous. Lomi also supplies many of the other cafés in the neighbourhood with coffee beans and offers workshops for budding baristas and latte artists in the school next door.

THE HARDWARE SOCIÉTÉ

10 rue Lamarck, 75018. +33 (0)1 42 51 69 03
**https://www.facebook.com/pages/
Hardware-Société/611299802368467**

The Parisian sister of the original version in Melbourne, this airy tiled space perched on the Butte Montmartre looks out across the city. Coffee, as you would expect, is exemplary and there's a fine choice of inventive brunch-style dishes, cakes and light bites.

SOUL KITCHEN

33 rue Lamarck, 75018. +33 (0)1 71 37 99 95
www.soulkitchenparis.fr

Tucked just behind the Sacré Cœur, this lovely little café offers a €13.90 lunchtime

menu with the likes of homemade cauliflower and tahini soup served with butternut squash focaccia plus brunch, cakes and more.

Do It Yourself

LA LAITERIE DE PARIS

74 rue des Poissonniers, 75018.
http://lalaiteriedeparis.blogspot.fr

Paris's first cheesemaker opened its doors in late 2017 – up until then France's hundreds of cheeses had traditionally been made locally to the herds that produce milk for them. The opening coincides with a renewed interest in consuming local produce and urban agriculture and locals are flocking to pick up fresh goats cheese finished with herbs or flower petals, yoghurts fermented on site and raw milk butter. Try Le Myrha, a pungent cow's milk cheese finished with beer from the local brewery, La Brasserie de la Goutte d'Or.

Cheeses made by the Laiterie de Paris, Paris's first cheesemaker. Helen Massy-Beresford

Helen Massy-Beresford

MARCHÉ COUVERT DE LA CHAPELLE (MARCHÉ DE L'OLIVE)

10 rue de l'Olive, 75018.
http://equipement.paris.fr/marche-couvert-la-chapelle-5522

On Sunday mornings this covered market is full of locals choosing a rôtisserie chicken for Sunday lunch. There's also a well-stocked cheese counter, Italian and Portuguese delicatessen counters, fruit and vegetable stalls, butchers and fishmongers. Stalls serving Thai dishes, Caribbean specialities and Moroccan couscous are a great option for a casual lunch.

EN VRAC

2 rue de l'Olive, 75018. +33 (0)1 53 26 03 94.
www.vinenvrac.fr

Buy your wine the environmentally-friendly way by filling up a reusable bottle from one of the huge stainless steel tanks that line the walls – cheaper for the consumer and better for the planet, according to Thierry Poincin, the wine merchant who decided to revive the old-fashioned way of buying wine – in bulk or en vrac. The selection of organic and natural wines from across France changes regularly and you can also choose from a selection of artisanal spirits – from rum to walnut liqueur – sold the same way.

BRASSERIE DE LA GOUTTE D'OR

28 rue de la Goutte d'Or, 75018. +33 (0)9 80 64 23 51.
http://www.brasserielagouttedor.com

Come and find out more about the locally brewed selection of craft beers, taste them accompanied by tapas on Fridays and Saturdays or buy some to take home.

FROMAGERIE LEPIC

20 rue Lepic, 75018. +33 (0)1 46 06 90 97
There's a superb variety of cheeses from across France and beyond at this wonderful cheesemonger, just one of dozens of food shops dotted along the winding rue Lepic – come for a browse and you'll come away with bags laden with goodies.

Helen Massy-Beresford

Perfect Pâtisseries

PAIN PAIN

88 rue des Martyrs, 75018. +33 (0)1 42 23 62 81
www.pain-pain.fr

This design-conscious pâtisserie and bakery brings a splash of colour and some zingy flavours to the grey cobbles of Montmartre – try a mango, rose, passion fruit and lychee éclair or the trademark

Zéphyr, a hazelnut and raspberry financier with white chocolate Chantilly cream infused with lime and vanilla.

LA ROSE DE TUNIS

7 boulevard Ornano, 75018. +33 (0)1 46 06 15 25

Authentic North African pastries in all their sticky, sesame-seeded glory are heaped high in the glass cabinets of this tiny bakery that caters to the area's large numbers of residents of North African origin.

Cosmopolitan Paris

LE DIBI

46 rue Polonceau, 75018. +33 (0)1 85 15 27 15.
www.restaurant-ledibi-paris18.fr

The Goutte d'Or district tucked away behind Montmartre isn't known as Little Africa for nothing. A wave of post-colonial immigration over the past decades has made it a hub of West African culture with a large market (rue Dejean) selling African ingredients and tiny textile shops piled high with traditional brightly coloured 'wax' fabrics. Although it doesn't look like much from the outside, Le Dibi is the place to go to try Senegalese mafé (peanut sauce), lemony yassa chicken (both at €10) and more.

TIM LA PRINCESSE

46 rue Marcadet, 75018. +33 (0)7 81 61 70 40

This tiny restaurant serves up delicacies from Ivory Coast including home-made

milk-based dégué dessert, with meal deals from €6.90. Eat at one of the tiny tables or take away.

NEW THAI SAN

44 rue de Torcy, 75018. +33 (0)1 42 09 23 18

You certainly don't go here for the friendly service – you'll likely have to queue for a cramped table and a fairly rushed canteen-style dining experience – but the mostly Asian clientele of New Thai San should be enough to convince you it's the real deal. The menu is almost overwhelmingly long but the Thai specialities are, as the name suggests, always a safe choice as are the rôtisserie dishes and the sautéed beef loc lac, a popular dish in Vietnam and Cambodia.

THU THU

51b rue Hermel, 75018. +33 (0)1 42 54 70 30

From the outside, this Vietnamese restaurant doesn't look like much, but inside, it's the real deal – try the banh cuon (steamed pork rolls), fragrant pho soup, pork with caramel or the beef loc lac, a spicy salad.

CAFÉ LÉON

50 rue Léon, 75018. +33 (0)1 42 54 43 39

Friendly neighbourhood café with a few pavement tables offering excellent cous cous and a selection of tapas.

19th Arrondissement

CRISS-CROSSED BY the Canal Saint-Martin and the Canal Saint-Denis, the 19th has a more spacious, airy feel than many Parisian arrondissements. There's a rough-and-ready vibe with many rundown streets, but the area is also home to some Paris gems which often go unnoticed by tourists sticking to the more central arrondissements: there's the wonderful Parc de la Villette made up of a huge canal-side park, the Cité de la musique concert space, the Zénith concert hall and the Cité des Sciences et de l'Industrie museum; the wonderfully landscaped Parc des Buttes-Chaumont which is carved out of an old quarry and the revitalised walkways around the Bassin de la Villette reservoir. Foodwise, many of the best options are concentrated around these three landmarks while with part of the Belleville 'Chinatown', one of two districts in the city with large numbers of Asian restaurants, falling in the 19th, noodles, nems and dim sum are on the menu too.

Pure Paris

AU BŒUF COURONNÉ

188 avenue Jean Jaurès, 75019. +33 (0)1 42 39 44 44

www.boeuf-couronne.com

Old meets new at the Bœuf Couronné where the proximity to La Villette's park, science museum and concert halls ensures a steady stream of diners (and guests – it's now a hotel too). As the name suggests, the impressive cuts of beef are what this place, which harks back to the old meat market in the area, is known for. If the 1.2 kg Villette beef rib steak for two at €74 is a challenge too far, thankfully the menu offers a selection of cuts for smaller appetites as well. Décor is brasserie style and there's a lovely comfortable outdoor seating area for sunny days.

LE LAUMIÈRE

4 rue Petit, 75019. +33 (0)1 42 02 46 71

www.laumiere.com

Fish and seafood are the specialities at this traditional and quite formal establishment near the Parc des Buttes-Chaumont (and with its own little garden) where the team is made up of veterans of some of the city's most famous brasseries. House specialities are the Louis XIV-style pike quenelles and bouillabaisse, a traditional fish stew originating from Marseille which you'll need to order ahead. There's a three-course set menu for €32.90.

CAFÉ BOLIVAR

31 avenue Secrétan, 75019. +33 (0)6 65 26 50 00
https://cafebolivar.fr/menu/

There's an enticing menu with regularly changing specials at this cosy neighbourhood bistrot where the décor is inviting and the service is friendly too.

Best Bistrots

QUEDUBON

22 rue du Plateau, 75019. +33 (0)1 42 38 18 65
www.restaurantquedubon.fr

Don't be put off by the somewhat off-the-beaten track location, Quedubon (just the good stuff) is what a Parisian bistrot should feel like, from the décor, all warm red walls lined with scrawled chalkboard menus and endless bottles of wine, to the food itself; bistronomy at its finest with ever-changing selections designed to highlight the best ingredients, for example a Salers steak simply cooked and served with braised little gem lettuce and lentils (€24). This is not an ideal place for vegetarians.

LE BASTRINGUE

67 quai de la Seine, 75019. +33 (0)1 85 15 22 97
www.lebastringue-paris.fr

An old-fashioned bistrot vibe, good value food – charcuterie platters at around €10, duck confit at €14.50 – and friendly service, all with the lovely view of the water beyond.

Al Fresco Paris

ROSA BONHEUR

Parc des Buttes-Chaumont, 2 avenue de la Cascade, 75019. +33 (0)1 42 00 00 45
http://rosabonheur.fr

In the glorious parc des Buttes-Chaumont, Rosa Bonheur is the perfect spot to tuck into a selection of wine, sweet and savoury tapas and wood-fired pizzas, with influences from the Camargue region of southern France. The Rosa Bonheur concept is a modern

Rosa Bonheur. Helen Massy-Beresford

guinguette – these were casual drinking and dancing establishments popular from the eighteenth century in the city's suburbs, most famously along the banks of the Marne. Parisians like the modern guinguette concept so much that two more branches of Rosa Bonheur have opened up – a floating Rosa Bonheur arrived on the Seine in 2013, and the latest incarnation, in the western suburb of Asnières-sur-Seine in 2017.

Helen Massy-Beresford

LE PAVILLON PUEBLA
39 avenue Símon Bolívar, 75019. +33 (0)1 42 39 34 20
www.leperchoir.tv

With hammocks, a shady terrace attached to a charming old house, cocktails and pizzas, DJs on weekend evenings and a kids' club on Sundays there's something for everyone here – and all within the bounds of the lush Parc des Buttes-Chaumont. What more could you ask for?

KIEZ KANAL
90 quai de la Loire, 75019, Paris. +33 (0)1 42 02 33 94
www.kiez.fr

The newest addition to the Kiez family, which is supplying thirsty Parisians with a selection of authentic German beers, wines and snacks is a few steps away from the Bassin de la Villette with a modern industrial-style interior and a little terrace that spills out onto the road. Currywurst and schnitzel, Paulaner and Bitburger on tap and a whole host of

bottled delights too – and a selection of German wine as well.

PANAME BREWING COMPANY
41bis quai de la Loire, 75019. + 33 (0) 1 40 36 43 55
www.panamebrewingcompany.com

The Paname Brewing Company (named after an old-fashioned nickname for Paris) is the perfect spot to grab a table

Helen Massy-Beresford

on the large terrace overlooking the water and work your way through the range of locally brewed craft beers and simple, hearty dishes such as ribs, pulled pork and stews. In the summer months a barbecue stall offers flame-grilled burgers.

BAR OURCQ
68 quai de la Loire, 75019. +33 (0)1 42 40 12 26
http://barourcq.free.fr
Grab a beer and borrow a set of boules from this laid-back neighbourhood bar to play on the boules ground outside next to the reservoir. Bar Ourcq is a casual hangout, with beer, wine and tapas the order of the day.

Martin Argyroglo

Pop-Up Paris

LA PETITE HALLE
211 avenue Jean Jaurès, 75019. +33 (0)9 82 25 91 81
www.lapetitehalle.com
Casual Italian with plenty of space and an outdoor (covered) terrace as well as that rare Parisian thing, a garden, in the Parc de la Villette. Great wood-fired pizzas, generous pasta dishes and more in a restaurant that doubles as a jazz venue.

LE CENTQUATRE-PARIS
5 rue Curial, 75019. +33 (0)1 53 35 50 00
www.104.fr
There are plenty of gourmet options in this eclectic and cavernous arts centre, where

Grand Central.

Marc Domage

you can come for an exhibition or talk or just to enjoy the vibrant atmosphere created by the small groups of street dancers and capoeira-fiends practising their routines in the large covered space. There are much sought-after wood-fired pizzas, crêpes and even mulled wine from the pizza truck or innovative brasserie-style fare from Le Grand Central, while Le Café Caché serves up fresh juices, cakes and simple snacks in a 1950s-inspired setting.

BIIIM
5-21 quai de la Loire, 75019. +33 (0)1 80 06 17 66
http://www.biiim.fr

Quality is a priority at this upmarket fast food joint attached to the canal-side MK2 cinema where the burgers, salads and hot dogs all have movie-themed names. You can check out the provenance of the meat and other ingredients on the poster just inside the door and the set meal deals, some of which are tied to buying cinema tickets too, are good value. Even à la carte, Biiim is reasonably priced, with main dishes at around €10. Try a locally-brewed beer from the Brasserie de la Goutte d'Or.

Café Culture
LE PAVILLON DES CANAUX
39 quai de la Loire, 75019. +33 (0)1 73 71 82 90
www.pavillondescanaux.com

Step back in time in this quirky vintage spot. Each room of the old house is imaginatively kitted out as a real room – you can sip your coffee in a 50s-style bathroom or enjoy one of the fresh soups or salads in the kitchen, should the fancy take you or on sunny days enjoy the view across the water from the conservatory. The Pavillon des Canaux is more than

just a café – it's a 'coffice' where laptop-workers are welcomed, as well as a social and cultural space. The events calendar includes everything from pop-up tattoo parlours to cooking and fitness classes as well as the inevitable weekend brunch – €24 for adults and €12 for children.

LE BELLERIVE
71 quai de la Seine, 75019. +33 (0)1 40 36 56 77

The terrace of this vintage haunt is a good spot for people- and boat-watching on a summer evening with a coffee or a glass of wine. Classic bistrot fare like beef bourguignon, steak tartare and grilled fish complete the picture.

Do It Yourself
HALLE SECRÉTAN
33 avenue Secrétan, 75019. +33 (0)1 40 05 10 79

This beautiful covered market, built in 1868, got a face lift a few years ago and is now home to an organic supermarket and a handful of other shops and restaurants.

LA CAVE DE BELLEVILLE
51 rue de Belleville, 75019. +33 (0)1 40 34 12 95
https://lacavedebelleville.wordpress.com

Come in to buy a bottle or stay and taste the wine (much of it organic, biodynamic or natural) in this welcoming wine and fine food emporium, accompanied by great bread and delicious cheese and charcuterie platters as well as some tasty tapas-style dishes. You can buy by the glass or pay a small corkage fee if you want to drink the bottle you've bought on site. If your French is up to it there are even wine-tasting workshops on offer.

Perfect Pâtisseries

LA VIEILLE FRANCE

5 avenue de Laumière, 75019. +33 (0)1 40 40 08 31

https://www.facebook.com/Pâtisserie-La-Vieille-France-745958312147243/

The name 'Old France' may seem appropriate at first glance but take a closer look and you'll see the Japanese influences – matcha and bean paste – in La Vieille France's delicious offerings.

POÎLANE

83 rue de Crimée, 75019.

www.poilane.com

The newest baby in the poîlane family: the baker famous for its sourdough has recently taken over this old-fashioned bakery complete with wood oven and vintage tiles and even pledged to keep making some of the fruit- and nut-studded loaves the previous owner was famous for.

Cosmopolitan Paris

GUO XIN

47 rue de Belleville, 75019. +33 (0)1 42 38 17 53

Come for the house speciality of dim sum at this diminutive Chinese restaurant in the heart of Belleville, Paris's second 'Chinatown' after the large Asian area in the 13th.

LE PACIFIQUE

35 rue de Belleville, 75019. +33 (0)1 42 49 66 80

Dim sum are the speciality at this vast, cavernous Chinese restaurant in the heart of the Belleville 'Chinatown' – don't be put off by the kitsch décor.

ITEGUE TAITU

66 rue Armand Carrel, 75019. +33 (0)1 42 82 11 47

http://iteguetaitu.com

Spicy and tasty Ethiopian specialities to share all served on the traditional injera buckwheat bread at this simple but enjoyable Ethiopian restaurant.

MIAN GUAN

34 rue de Belleville, 75019. +33 (0)1 40 33 45 01

A Chinatown favourite, Mian Guan serves up huge bowls of nourishing homemade noodle soups to a hungry local clientele.

BOMBAY CURRY

119 rue de Meaux, 75019. +33 (0)1 42 40 41 38

www.bombay-curry.fr

A great option for vegetarians, with plenty of meat-free choices, this friendly neighbourhood Indian restaurant is perfect for a hit of spice.

23

20th Arrondissement

AMONG THE TWENTY Parisian arrondissements, the 20th is perhaps the one that has best managed to retain its village-vibe, even while increasingly becoming the district of choice for artists, writers and other creative types. Perhaps it's La Campagne à Paris (the countryside in Paris), a rare island of houses and leafy gardens in an intensely built-up city of mostly tall apartment buildings. Or the quaint streets around the Saint-Germain de Charonne church where you feel as if you've stepped back in time to a lost Paris. Or the Père Lachaise cemetery, the largest in Paris and the wonderfully picturesque resting place of some of the city's most famous former residents – Jim Morrison, Édith Piaf, Oscar Wilde and Marcel Proust to name but a few. Nowadays, the 20th is home to a young and creative population tempted out of the more central Parisian districts by cheaper rents – and the exodus has created a buzzing area of shops and restaurants clustered around the place Gambetta and beyond.

Pure Paris

LES CANAILLES MÉNILMONTANT

15 rue des Panoyaux, 75020. +33 (0)1
www.les-canailles-menilmontant.com

Set in a former 1930s brasserie – the space retains many of the charming original features – this little sister for Les Canailles Pigalle (in the 9th at 25 rue La Bruyère) highlights the success of the original. Both seek to create a warm and inviting atmosphere evoking a Paris of days gone by. The menu too harks back to traditional French favourites, adding a foam here and an exotic ingredient there to bring them bang up to date. There are set menus at €28 for two courses and €35 for three and an express weekday lunch menu at €17/19.

LE BISTROT DU PARISIEN

31 rue Pelleport, 75020. +33 (0)1 43 61 07 91
https://www.facebook.com/Le-Bistro-Du-Parisien-301528833286716/

Hearty traditional dishes – think bone marrow and simply grilled steaks

Le Bistrot du Parisien

Le Bistrot du Parisien

although there are some lighter options such as goat's cheese salad – perfectly executed in a warm and cosy atmosphere.

LES ALLOBROGES

71 rue des Grands Champs, 75020. +33 (0)1 43 73 40 00

Fine-dining in a formal dining room, with the emphasis on the best ingredients from across France.

Best Bistrots

CAFÉ LE PAPILLON

144 rue de Bagnolet, 75020. +33 (0)1 43 73 38 55
www.cafelepapillon.com

Delicate and colourful platefuls are on the menu at Le Papillon, a pretty little address in the 20th, where sitting at one of the pavement tables for a drink is a nice way to while away an hour or two as well.

LE GRAND BAIN

14 rue Dénoyez, 75020. +33 (0)9 83 02 72 02
www.legrandbainparis.com

British chef Edward Delling-Williams and his team are on to a winner at Le Grand Bain where Parisians flock for small, perfectly presented sharing plates buzzing with flavour: the likes of asparagus and wild garlic (€7) or razor clams with salsa verde (€6). Some dishes are not so small: try the succulent lamb shoulder (€45) or whole trout (€15) if they are on offer. Natural wines and craft beers and a lovely airy dining room complete the picture.

LE PETIT 20E

381 rue des Pyrénées, 75020. +33 (0)1 43 49 34 50
www.petit20.com

This neighbourhood bistrot promises local and seasonal ingredients cooked with flair and its short menu certainly delivers. It's slightly out of the way but that's reflected in the very reasonable prices – starters around €10 and main courses just under €20.

DILIA

1 rue d'Eupatoria, 75020. +33 (0)9 53 56 24 14
www.dilia.fr

High quality bistronomy with an Italian twist in a tiny but welcoming setting.

Helen Massy-Beresford

LES TRIPLETTES

102 boulevard de Belleville, 75020. +33 (0)1 43 15 09 54
https://www.facebook.com/ Lestriplettesbelleville/

A constantly changing menu of daily specials at €16 for three courses plus a happy hour every evening.

LE COMPTOIR

30 rue Villiers de l'Isle Adam, 75020. +33 (0)9 84 55 25 63
https://www.facebook.com/ lecomptoirgambetta/

A short weekly-changing menu and a fine selection of wines to go with it at this neighbourhood wine bar/bistrot.

LE JOURDAIN

101 rue des Couronnes, 75020. +33 (0)1 43 66 29 10
https://www.facebook.com/ restaurantlejourdain

Original and flavourful tapas dishes with a focus on seafood at this tiny neighbourhood place – booking is advisable.

AUX PETITS OIGNONS

11 rue Dupont de l'Eure, 75020. +33 (0)1 43 64 18 86
http://auxpetitsoignonsparis.fr

A typical Parisian bistrot with atmosphere, charm and old-school, good quality food – classic dishes are executed perfectly. In summer try one of the few outdoor pavement tables.

Al Fresco Paris

MONCŒUR BELLEVILLE

1 rue des Envierges, 75020. +33 (0)1 43 66 38 54
www.moncoeurbelleville.com

You can't argue with Moncœur Belleville's claim that it has one of Paris's most beautiful terraces, its position on the Ménilmontant hill giving it a panoramic view across the city. Come for a good value and original brunch at the weekend or raise a glass to the backdrop of a sparkling Eiffel Tower in the evening. This venue has changed hands several times over the past decade – its latest iteration is the best. The menu changes daily but

Mama Shelter

Moncœur Belleville.

flavours are always fresh and original, not to mention good value, with daily specials at €12 and a 3-course 'formule' at €17.50. Weekend brunch is worth the wait (bookings are for groups of six or more only) – the sometimes eclectic selection of dishes that make up a Parisian brunch complement each other well here. All this, and it also has one of the best views over Paris.

MAMA SHELTER
109 rue de Bagnolet, 75020. +33 (0)1 43 48 48 48.
www.mamashelter.com

In stark (no pun intended) contrast to this formerly somewhat sleepy corner of the 20th arrondissement, Philippe Starck-designed Mama Shelter is a beacon of urban cool, with hotel rooms, a restaurant and a lively agenda of events. The rooftop bar, voted the best in Paris by Vogue in 2017, is a wonderful asset with lounge-worthy sofas illuminated by fairy lights and ping-pong tables for the more energetic. There genuinely is something for everyone on the extensive menu – from Poke Bowls to pizzas to sharing plates as well as brunch at the weekends (€44 per head).

Going Green

LOVE ME CRU
44 rue de Tourtille, 75020. +33 (0)1 71 93 08 26
https://www.facebook.com/lovemecru/

Organic, vegan, raw and gluten-free – but full of flavour: soup, salads, wraps, juices and more all served with a smile in this tiny space.

PRIMEUR
4 rue Lemon, 75020. +33 (0)1 71 70 95 28
https://www.facebook.com/cantineprimeur/

Colourful salad bowls, lentil burgers, spring rolls, stir fries and to finish off, vegan cashew 'cheesecake' at this simple but tasty veggie café.

LE MEZZE DU CHEF

80 rue de Ménilmontant, 75020. +33 (0)6 95 65 19 20

Come here for the çig-köfte, a traditional dish in south-eastern Turkey originally made with raw meat but now transformed into the perfect vegetarian lunch: bulgur, walnuts, pepper, onion, garlic and tomatoes as well as 27 spices and a dash of pomegranate syrup are the main ingredients. Try it as a sandwich for €4 or as part of a platter at €10. There are vegetarian mezze too as well as sticky-sweet baklava to finish.

Pop-Up Paris

CHEZ ELLE

3 rue des Tourelles, 75020. +33 (0)1 40 31 12 10
www.chezellerestaurant.free.fr

A vintage 70s vibe sets the tone in this happy-go-lucky neighbourhood joint, with a little selection of toys for visiting children and a daily-changing special at lunchtime. In the evening, drinks are accompanied by generous charcuterie and cheese platters.

LA HALLE AUX OLIVIERS – LA BELLEVILLOISE

19-21 rue Boyer, 75020. +33 (0)1 46 36 07 07
www.labellevilloise.com

Neo-bistrot flavours mix with notes of jazz, folk and more in the green and airy setting of La Bellevilloise, originally Paris's first cooperative and now a lively arts and music venue. There's a jazz brunch on Sundays and public holidays.

Café Culture

LA MÈRE LACHAISE

78 boulevard de Ménilmontant, 75020.
+33 (0)9 86 57 95 10
www.lamerelachaise.com

Regular concerts, exhibitions and themed brunches attract a lively crowd to this casual café, as does its setting on the broad expanse of pavement on the boulevard, with plenty of space for al fresco drinking and eating in the summer months. There's a pretty classic but reliable menu of the likes of steaks, salads and grilled fish too.

AUX FOLIES BELLEVILLE

8 rue de Belleville, 75020. +33 (0)6 28 55 89 40
http://www.aux-folies-belleville.fr/contact.php

A typically Parisian and very lively café/bar that's something of an institution in this mixed area – part gentrifying young professionals, part old-fashioned working class neighbourhood. The name is a reference to the cabaret where Édith Piaf – who was born in the area – used to sing.

LA LAVERIE

1 rue de Ménilmontant, 75020. +33 (0)1 43 66 39 64

A lively neighbourhood café-bistrot with a pleasant terrace looking out onto the winding rue Ménilmontant and a good, simple menu.

Do It Yourself

MAISON LANDEMAINE
210 rue des Pyrénées, 75020. +33 (0)1 43 49 36 89

www.maisonlandemaine.com

The queue outside this bakery speaks for itself. As well as the usual range of baguettes, sourdough loaves and seeded breads there's an exquisite selection of beautiful pâtisseries, fruit tarts with perfectly flaky pastry and specialities including fougasse (olive-oil infused bread from Provence), and kouglof (an Alsatian sweet speciality bread full of raisins). There are branches dotted across Paris ... and there's even one in Tokyo. Closed on Wednesdays.

L'ÉPICERIE Ô DIVIN
130 rue de Belleville, 75020. +33 (0)1 43 66 62 63

https://www.facebook.com/o.divin.paris/

You'll find top quality ingredients and luxury food items in this trendy neighbourhood grocery store. There's a greengrocer's in the same street at 128 and a fishmonger's at 118.

Perfect Pâtisseries

DEMONCY-VERGNE
10 rue du Jourdain, 75020. +33 (0)1 46 36 66 08

https://www.demoncy-vergne.com

Try the prize-winning millefeuille at this charming pastry shop.

LE 140
140 rue de Belleville, 75020. +33 (0)1 46 36 92 47.

www.au140.com

The wood-fired oven is the secret to the amazing variety and quality of bread at this neighbourhood bakery, while the buttery viennoiseries and tarts made with seasonal fruits are well worth a try too.

Cosmopolitan Paris

WEN ZHOU
16 rue de Belleville, 75020.

Cheap and cheerful Chinese canteen-style dining – come for the good value flavoursome dishes and not for the service which is basic or for the atmosphere: cramped.

CHEZ YOUNICE
13 rue d'Avron, 75020. +33 (0)1 43 56 84 38

www.chez-younice.fr/

Cheap and cheerful good quality and authentic Moroccan cuisine.